MORE LIVES THAN ONE

Mark Jenkins was born in London of Irish and Welsh parents. He was educated at Highbury Grammar School and then drafted into the army, after which he read Politics and Economics at the University of Westminster and the LSE. He taught at West Ham and South Thames Colleges, before moving to Cardiff to take up the post of Principal Lecturer in Policy Studies at the University of Glamorgan, though nowadays he teaches students on the MA Scriptwriting course. As a member of Amnesty International's Russian section, he assisted in the release of several leading Soviet dissidents. Mark is widely published and his plays have been performed around the world. His first feature film, *The Scarlet Tunic*, starring Simon Callow, Emma Fielding and Jean-Marc Barre, premiered at Cannes and at the Leicester Square Odeon, London, before national release.

MORE LIVES THAN ONE

FIVE PLAYS

MARK JENKINS

PARTHIAN

Parthian
The Old Surgery
Napier Street
Cardigan
SA43 1ED

www.parthianbooks.co.uk

ISBN 1-902638-41-7

Cover design by Marc Jennings
Printed and bound by Dinefwr Press, Llandybie, Wales
Typeset in Sabon by type@lloydrobson.com

Parthian is an independent publisher which works with the support
of the Welsh Books Council and the Arts Council of Wales

British Library Cataloguing in Publication Data. A cataloguing
record for this book is available from the British Library

In memory of my mother
Catherine Alice Fleming
1913-1987

'He who leads more lives than one,
more deaths than one must die'

Oscar Wilde, The Ballad of Reading Gaol

CONTENTS

Author's Preface   xiii
Production Histories   xv
Acknowledgements   xvii

Playscripts

Playing Burton   1
Birthmarks   35
Downtown Paradise   121
Mr Owen's Millennium 181
Nora's Bloke   203

Mark Jenkins In Conversation
With Hazel Walford Davies   271
Review Excerpts   283

AUTHOR'S PREFACE

The title of this selection is taken from Oscar Wilde's *The Ballad of Reading Gaol* – 'He who leads more lives than one, more deaths than one must die.' The quotation provides a unifying theme for the five works included here.

The plays depict many lives. All are about people who actually lived and, with the exception of *Nora's Bloke*, they are all historical figures of some stature – Richard Burton, Karl Marx, Robert Owen and a more obscure American lawyer, whom I call 'Rachel Bloom'. The subjects could, additionally, be said to have lived 'more lives than one' in the sense that 'one man in his time plays many parts'; and, also, because their 'lives' and deaths are re-enacted by actors, interpreting the roles devised for them. Consider Julius Caesar, who has been done to death more times than he might care to suffer, both by pen and wooden sword! It is a posthumous hazard of the famous, that in their immortality, they must die more deaths than one.

'Raising the dead' is nothing new in drama. Playwrights have been doing it for centuries. Exclusive obsession with the contemporary can become a form of narcissism. At its worst, it can degenerate into social engineering or the peddling of worthy causes and politically 'correct' prejudices. The artist must be able to stand well back from his canvas if he is to escape the tyranny of immediate impressions. The present we inhabit is every bit as fraught with the difficulties of perception as the 'done and dusted' past. Both past and present are replete with uncertainties and subject to our continual re-interpretations of 'reality'.

And so, the dramatist needs a set of guidelines for his researches. Mine are as follows: primary sources (what historical figures are recorded as actually having done or said) must take precedence over secondary sources (interpretations by commentators), especially where the two conflict; refrain from attributing to real-life characters actions and opinions they are known not to have committed or expressed; in grey areas between verifiable fact and surmise, remain true to the logic and spirit of the character as revealed in primary sources.

These rules are not fail-safe, however. 'Facts' are slippery customers. 'The truth is rarely pure and never simple' (Wilde, again). Dramatic truth, if it is to have revelatory power, should be honestly rooted in historical evidence, which may have been overlooked or even deliberately concealed. For instance, Marx's paternity of his housekeeper's illegitimate son, Freddy Demuth, was conspiratorially suppressed for over one hundred years by those who feared it would compromise the purity of the image of their prophet. Likewise, Marx's own morbid anti-Semitism was incredibly rationalised by his followers as a mere metaphor for 'anti-capitalism'.

In *Birthmarks*, I suggest it was a pathological condition, producing psychosomatic physical ailments (his boils and carbuncles) every time he investigated what he called 'the Jewish essence' of capital. In 'On the Jewish Question', Marx's anti-Semitism is explicit and systematised, but the work is seldom read.

The purpose of these plays, therefore, is not iconoclasm, but, hopefully, a greater insight into the true humanity and, thereby, drama of the subjects' lives, as revealed in often marginal episodes.

PRODUCTION HISTORIES

Playing Burton was written in Pontypridd, in 1986. It was first produced by David Bidmead at the Etcetera Theatre, Camden, North London, in the autumn of 1992, with Josh Richards starring. The director responsible for its initial success was Hugh Thomas, one of Wales' leading directorial talents in both theatre and television, who kindly financed the costly rehearsals. It then toured numerous venues in England and Wales for two years.

In 1994, Josh Richards was again the performer when Richard Burton's great-nephew, director and producer Guy Masterson, took the show to Edinburgh, where it drew standing ovations and won outstanding reviews before touring worldwide, returning to a sell-out run at Edinburgh in 1997. Since then it has toured in London, Stratford-on-Avon, Tel Aviv, Budapest, Brisbane, Sydney (Opera House), Wellington, Auckland, Christchurch, Cape Cod (USA) and most recently, for ten weeks in autumn 2003, in New York City. Four actors currently play the role for various companies on three continents: Welshman, Josh Richards; Englishman, George Telfer; New Zealander, Ray Henwood (who won New Zealand's 'Actor of the Year' award in the role), and Irish-American, Brian Mallon. All have received accolades for their performances as Richard Burton.

This current volume is the second publication of the play by Parthian Books.

Birthmarks, the author's first play, was written in Pontypridd, in 1985. It won first prize out of 120 entries in both languages, in a national competition organised by the Drama Association of Wales in December 1986. Nevertheless, it initially failed to get a production in Wales. The first, low-budget, production was for two weeks at the Taurus Theatre Club in North London, in May 1987, by Buzz Theatre Company, director: Richard Leggatt.

The second, funded, production was two years later, in April-May 1989, by Cardiff Everyman Theatre in association with WOT Theatre. Director: Jeremy James. Lead parts starred Laurence Llewellyn, Tim May, Cler Stephens and Alison Jenkins. It played for two weeks at Chapter Arts Centre's main stage and then toured to Theatr Tri-bühne, Stuttgart, Baden-Wurtemburg, (West) Germany, funded by Cardiff City Council and Stuttgart's Town Council. Mayor Rommel gave a special reception for the company. Two months later, quite by chance, the Berlin wall came down!

Downtown Paradise was written in Canton, Cardiff, in 1995. It, too, was turned down by Welsh companies. It was first produced by Tim Williams and the Drama Audit company (later Out of Wales), financed by a consortium of London accountants. It ran for six weeks at The Finborough Theatre, Chelsea, in April-May 1996. Sarah Esdaile directed. Amanda Hurwitz and Black-American actor, Richard C Sharp, starred. It then transferred to the Chapter Arts Centre, Cardiff, for a further two weeks.

Mr Owen's Millennium, written in Pontypridd, in 1985-86, was developed as a stage play from the author's own Welsh-translated television drama *Er Gwell; Er Gwaith*, directed by Wil Aaron of Nant Films and broadcast on S4C, in 1985. Unable to secure a Welsh theatrical production, it was contracted by David Bidmead to run for three weeks in the second London Festival of Solo shows at the Etcetera Theatre, Camden, before transferring to Chapter Arts Centre in January 1997. The actor who played the role of Owen, to great acclaim, was Owen Garmon. Special thanks go to Steve Fisher, the director, who did a magnificent job of editing an over-long script and providing a highly imaginative set design.

Nora's Bloke, written in Cardiff, in 1994, began its public life as a short story for a 1995 'love story' competition, organised by the South Wales Echo. Novelist Iris Gower awarded the author the first prize of a word processor and Nora was published. In 2001 it was re-written as a one-act play for a script-in-hand performance at Dempsey's theatre bar, Cardiff, directed by the author. Then, during a preliminary spring 2002 USA tour of *Playing Burton*, the author was approached by a resident company, based at the New York Irish Arts Centre, looking for a play to perform. *Nora's Bloke* was gratefully received and, at the company's request, further developed as a two-act play. This new version was first performed, script-in-hand, at the New York Irish Arts Centre, in August 2002. In December 2003, it was produced by Cardiff Everyman Theatre for a pre-Christmas run at Llanover Hall Arts Centre, Cardiff, directed by the author.

ACKNOWLEDGEMENTS

Playing Burton includes quotes from Richard Burton and the works of Edward Albee, William Dunbar, T S Eliot, Christopher Hampton, John Le Carré, Christopher Marlowe, George Orwell, William Shakespeare, Dylan Thomas.

Thanks to:

Producers Richard Leggatt of Buzz Theatre Company, London; David Bidmead of Etcetera Theatre Company, London; Jeremy James of WOT Theatre Company, Cardiff; Everyman Theatre Company, Cardiff; Phil Setren of London New Play Festival; Tim Williams of Drama Audit Theatre Company, London, and private financial backers from the Audit Commission; Guy Masterson of Masterson Productions, London; James Hanlon of Redbranch Productions, New York City; Ray Henwood of Circa Theatre Productions, Christchurch, New Zealand; Paul Maury and Thomas Egedal of Nordiska Strakosch Teaterforgalet, Copenhagen, Denmark.

Directors Richard Leggatt, Jeremy James, Hugh Thomas, Guy Masterson, Steve Fisher, Sarah Esdaile, Aretha Breeze.

Also, Wil Aaron, Sam Boardman-Jacobs, Sean Burke, Jeremy Davies, Lewis Davies, Daniel Figuero, Steve Fisher, Owen Garmon, Jon Gower, Ray Henwood, David Hughes, Judith Isherwood, Elaine James, Lewis James, Zygi Kamasa, Brian Mallon, Alan Osborne, Robin Reeves, Francesca Rhydderch, Josh Richards, Lloyd Robson, Phil Setren, George Telfer, Hazel Walford Davies, and Tim Williams, for all their help and encouragement.

Special thanks go to former BBC Wales producer and director, Brian Turvey.

PLAYING BURTON

First performed by Josh Richards, directed by Hugh Thomas; and subsequently by Ray Henwood, directed by Guy Masterson; George Telfer, directed by Adrian Lloyd-James; and Brian Mallon, directed by the author.

ACT ONE

Music of Camelot swells to the 'bong' of Big Ben. Lights to black. It is the start of the BBC News announcing Burton's death, then the announcer starts a résumé of Burton's life. When the announcer says 'This marked the beginning of his lifelong association with Elizabeth Taylor' we hear a voice in the dark and see Richard light a match and cigarette. Pinspot up on Richard.

No! Stop. I'm not ready for that! I will not go gentle into that good night!

Announcement stops.

Oh no! *Wild men who caught and sang the sun in flight, and learn, too late, they grieved it on its way, do not go gentle into that good night.* Who's out there? God? Mephistopheles? Darryl F Zanuck? (*Lights fade up. He looks at the table, chair, and vodka, and suddenly sees the audience.*) Ah, the faces in the dark. The expectant faces. Perhaps that's all there ever was. Fingers caught in the emotional till and now a reckoning?

It was all going to happen for me, and I knew it. But not why. I was aware that my people had nothing, yet I wanted for nothing. It seemed like providence. But I did not know.

I was filled with wonder; a sense of destiny which trampled over circumstance, as if to some purpose. Death had robbed me of my mother's love, yet I was loved to death by all my sisters. Oh, I was spoilt with love! I lost two sisters on the way. So still, like undivined jewels trapped in cold black stone. I could have been one of them. They perished; I did not. When my brothers were hungry, they set food before me on the table. They laboured in darkness while I stretched my arms up to the sunlight.

What is the purpose of it all? Why me play Richard; wear the crown? No one has ever been able to explain that to me. And what is this 'talent' I possess? Some call it 'a gift'. I find that unsatisfactory. Why give to one and not another?

What is it they say about a gift? 'It's the thought that counts?' The thought. Or lack of it! If there is anything at all behind creation it is not thought, or love, morality, or meaning, and surely not 'benevolence' – a kind of arbitrary force which scatters love, pain, joy, death, 'gifts' at will. An endless, random, game of dice. Good and evil become two sides of the same confusion.

I feel a great stillness within me. People say it shows on stage. Yes. A stillness. Why me play Richard? If there's a God, then he was drunk at my conception, just like my father. Drunk, too, for most of his eternity! So, you see, I wanted, needed, to be closer to what made me who I am. And, at last, for a few brief shining moments, I felt as though appearances were falling away, and I could reclaim myself for myself.

I've wanted desperately to play Lear for two or three years, but my neck was broken, and you can't play Lear in that condition. The King has to lift a young woman in his arms – difficult, with a perforated ulcer and one's entire spinal column coated with crystallised alcohol. They had to open me up and scrape it all off with a scalpel. Lear is a Welshman – 'Llŷr' in Welsh. The word 'England' is never mentioned in the play. Lear is King of Britain. Shakespeare is writing about pre-Anglo-Saxon Britain. He deliberately mangles the language. It's wrought, and taut, and strangled.

Some of the lines are unspeakable, but they have to be said. It's as if Shakespeare's tearing himself apart. It would be nice to play him in the English theatre, but English theatre is so boring these days. Broadway is infinitely more exciting. If you're opening at eight pm, by one o'clock in the morning you know whether to catch the next flight out because it's dead, cut, finished. Now, at the Royal Shakespeare you can play for an entire season with bad notices. People will still come. Why? Because it's the Royal. I don't think that's interesting. You should have to fight the way Edmund Keane had to fight; David Garrick; Henry Irving. Did I fight?

In Lear's own kingdom they speak the language of Heaven, the language I was brought up in. My parents in the chapel spoke the language of King Llŷr and I'm bilingual to this day. At home with friends sometimes I surprise an English guest by slipping into it. It isn't for effect. It's me. It's us.

I can remember – I must have been eight or nine – one day reading a poem in a foreign language in an old yellowing book with pages falling out. It was under the heading 'English Literature' and I could feel the strength and beauty of this foreign tongue. All that I have done, I have done in a language that was not my own.

My mother died when I was two. My eldest sister, Cis, brought me up. Now my sister was no ordinary woman – no woman ever is, but to me, my sister less than any. She, my sister, became my mother and more mother to me than any mother ever could have been. I was immensely proud of her. I shone in the reflection of her green-eyed, black-haired, gypsy beauty. She sang at her work in a voice so pure that the local men said she had a bell in every tooth and was gifted by God. She was innocent and guileless and infinitely protectable. She was naïve to the point of saintliness, and wept a lot at the misery of others. She felt all tragedies except her own.

I had read of the knights of chivalry and I knew that I had a bounden duty to protect her above all other creatures. It wasn't until thirty years later, when I saw her in another woman, that I realised that I had been searching for her all my life.

Cis and Ifor – guardians of the Milky Way of my childhood. Ifor – my brother and a father. Nineteen years my senior. He was twenty-nine when I was ten, light years in the timeless dust of a small boy's universe. Ifor straddled my firmament like a great bear. God-like hewer of coal; steadfast husband; fearsome, front row forward of the local rugby team. He was my lodestar, my Roy Rogers, my Joe Louis. I wanted to be the man my brother was.

I had a Welsh accent you could cut with a knife. However I was fourteen, and left school early to help Cis with my beer and cigarettes. Know what my ambition was? To squat on my haunches on a Saturday street corner with the ankles of my trousers bound with string, and my blue scarred miner's arms folded 'cross my chest to show the mark of a man, chewing on a matchstick to impress the girls, and whistling as they passed. Half a crown in my pocket to swill the coal dust from my belly. Oh my horizons were... lower than the horizon.

I could have been buried alive with my boyhood boyos, digging themselves deeper into darkness until their bodies turned to coal, unadored in their brief and gentle manliness. How many Burton baritones have gone unsung, above them the earth? And that's what I thought I wanted, to be below with them.

In the meantime I settled for the worst of all worlds: I worked in the gentlemen's outfitters department of the Co-op store. Haberdashery. Shabby! One morning I was cleaning brass on the shop door when along came my old teacher, Meredith Jones. Now, you didn't mess with Meredith Jones....

'Mornin'.'

'What are you doing, Jenkins?'

'What do you think? Cleaning the bastard brass!'

He clipped me round the ear and told me not to speak with a cigarette in my mouth.

'But I've left school now, Mr Jones!'

'No you haven't. You're just about to start, immediately, understand?'

It was the hardest thing I'd done in my life. A drop-out going back to school. No! Even harder were those voice sessions with Philip Burton, every evening until ten o'clock....

'Now how seriously do you want to be an actor, Jenkins?'

'Very serious, Mr Buurt'n, I've never been more serious. I'll work, work harder, harder than I've ever done. I know I can do it!'

But that time I first read Hamlet for him....

'Here, Jenkins, read this.'

'Tobe or Noddwbe; thaad is the qweschan
Wheatha tis norbla in the maend to suffer
The slings an' arroz of aoutrajus forchewn
Or to take aarms against a seee of trubble....'

'Kindly pause for a moment, Jenkins, I think I need a large sherry.'

'Do you laek it Mr Buurt'n?'

'I used to Jenkins, I used to like it. Tell me, do you know what the words mean?'

'Oh aye, I mean, yes, Mr Buurt'n.'

'Then tell me what the Prince is thinking in this piece.'

'I think the Prince... is in two minds. I think he's trying to work out what to do with his life. Whether to 'take arms against a sea of trouble' – the obstacles that confront 'im, 'and by opposing, end them' – change his situation for the better, instead of dithering, you know, take hold of things. You know, master his own destiny.'

There was a long pause. He looked at me fondly, put his hand on my shoulder and said 'Well done, Richard. Now I think we can start.'

I courted you, Philip. Not you; me. I needed to get close to you. In the blitz, on fire-watching duty, who first suggested I move in with you? When you took an interest in me, I could feel the wind filling my sails.

Wild Jenks at seventeen – boxing poet with a magic uncle! Salvaged from six months of living hell in haberdashery, from a cul-de-sac of long johns! Wild Jenks – closet ciggy smoker in a vanishing playground; boozy scholar; boy of many parts. Peeing from train windows as we rattled through a platform of spellbound passengers – my first public appearance in Wales!

I had a wild ambition to go out into the world and starve for something beautiful. Become a preacher: I'd show you sin in a posy of primroses, and redemption in a barmaid's thighs; innocence in an old man's laughter; and true companionship in a good, clean scrap. I'd recreate the world in seven words with a few, well-tuned, silences.

I am in love with vowels. Knocked out by consonants. I believe they were made for each other and I was made for them. I want to dwell with them forever on dusty coal-tips, along the charmed embankments of the railways and on the viaducts of heaven! I want to be the authentic voice of the Valley of the Shadow of Coal; the deep, dark voice of real men, whose life is work and who deserve no less than hold the centre of the stage.

No! I'll play for Wales! Win a cap! Don the Red Jersey! Do battle with the English enemy.... 'Yes, here he comes, the new cap from Pontrhydyfen... along the touch-line... dummies one man... two men... he's going for the gap! He's over! Superb in its creation. This young man who only last week won the Welsh Youth Light Middleweight Championship is faced with a difficult choice: rugby, boxing, poetry, preacher, or Prime Minister!'

Yes, there's a lot you don't know about me. Even more I don't know about myself. Do you remember when you were a kid with the evening sun at your back and the rest of time before you, and from your feet there sprouts forth this... colossal shadow of yourself? And every step bestrides a mountainside. You're like a puppet master with a giant hanging densely from your strings, yet light as air! One finger raised becomes a gesture of the infinite – and the sky is silence. You can take it, take it all! One day my shadow just... cut loose and bounded off across an ocean and a continent, and left that little kid with empty strings. A boy without a shadow. Yes, if he wanted to follow me, Little Jenks would have to change his name, give up the language of his birth, trade in his father, and hide himself behind a mask, take on a thousand parts within a labyrinth of words. Lose himself to find himself.

Philip taught me how to dress; what to wear for different occasions; how to conduct myself in public; which knife and fork to use; how to take soup without sound effects; and how to eat as though each meal were not my last!

Philip taught me to use English like a sword. Not that mincing nanny-goat 'Oxford English' in which 'man' and 'men' dissolve away to 'meahn'. All consonants were liberated like 'as-k-ed' and 'dep-th-s', and this enriched the vowels. It was emancipation. What he revealed I grew to love and... I became my teacher's son. Moved in with him and took his name. He was committed to me; and all he did, he did for love of me.

Oxford. It's taken a world war and the RAF to get me in. It's like a foreign country. Fellows – all airs and graces – but not above borrowing money off me. 'By Jove, you've played Emlyn Williams on the West End stage? I say, you couldn't lend me a fiver, could you?'

Neville Coghill makes me understudy for the part of 'Angelo'. I can miss drill and grow my hair long.

One day, Angelo vanishes. I go on, and West End impresario, 'Binky' Beaumont comes to see me in performance. Loves me!

'You absolutely must come to see me in London, darling, when this beastly war is over.' So, when the beastly war is over, darlings, I do, and he signs me up immediately. Ten pounds a week. A fortune!

How does a Prince become a King? I spend the war discussing these strategic matters with Robert Hardy and Warren Mitchell in local pubs, between rugby matches. Now, take the two parts of Henry the Fourth and Henry the Fifth as one piece. Prince Hal is all three. As separate plays, the prince is overshadowed by Hotspur in part one and Falstaff in part two. Lo and behold the wretched boy becomes King in the last play. But see it as a whole. See the Prince as apprentice. Now you've got three very different plays: Hal working his way from backstreet pubs, to the throne; Hal ready to take on the world. The perfect part.

And, after working for Binky Beaumont and landing a film contract, it happens! I'm ready to take on Stratford, where, according to Kenneth Tynan, I carry my own cathedral on with me, in which I am 'spotted' by Humphrey Bogart and Lauren Bacall – Lo and behold! – who duly report back to the powers that be in jolly old Hollywood, and then – Cry God for Richard – Broadway, and DARRYL F ZANUCK!

I'm loaned to Mr Zanuck. I have no say in it. He stars me in 'My Cousin Rachel' and 'The Robe'. They do so well he insists he has me under contract, and then he sues me. On one side of the courtroom, Darryl Zanuck and half the corporation boys in America. On the other side, me, alone – no lawyer. I play it very English, very Ronald Coleman. Suddenly, one of the lawyers jumps up, shakes his fist at me, 'You shook hands with Mr Zanuck on this agreement. You shook hands with Mr Zanuck in his own office.'

I reply, 'I don't believe Mr Zanuck said that because he's an honourable man. But if he did say it, then he's a fucking liar.'

The place breaks up in confusion. Strong men faint and are carried off by weak men. The next morning, the phone rings. There's a woman on the end of it.

'Did you call Darryl Zanuck a fucking liar?'

'Yes I think I did.'

'Then you need help, I'll be right over.'

She becomes my first legal adviser. It's now a very different world.

Zanuck simply couldn't understand why I should want to quit Hollywood to play Hamlet at the Old Vic for forty-five a week. Well it takes some explaining. He held up his hands, 'Old Vic? Who is this guy? Is he family? He wants money? So, I'll give him money!'

My first party at a swank house in the Bel Air district of Los Angeles. Sunbathing by the pool – Kirk Douglas and Hedy Lamar, drinking highballs, iced beer, wet brown arms reach out of the pool, shake my paw.

'Hi there Dick!'

'Don't call me Dick,' I say, 'Makes me feel like some kind of symbol.'

I am enjoying this small social triumph when a girl sitting on the other side of the pool lowers her book, takes off her sunglasses and looks at me with such... coolness... a new ice cube forms in my Scotch & Soda. She is so extraordinarily beautiful I nearly laugh out loud. A combination of plenitude, frugality, abundance, tightness. She sips some beer, and goes back to her book! She is totally ignoring me, not interested in talking, not yet. Not for some time yet.

Take this of me, Kate of my consolation
Hearing thy mildness praised in every town
Thy virtues spoke of and thy beauty sounded
Yet not so deeply as to thee belongs,
Myself am moved to woo thee for my wife.
And will you, nil you, I will marry you...
Now Kate, I am a husband for your turn;
For, by this light whereby I see thy beauty,
Thy beauty doth make me like thee well,
Thou must be married to no man but me....

After my first year in Hollywood, marauding bands of taxmen began raids along my coastline. Each spring they anchored in the Thames and in Port Talbot bay, wading ashore with briefcases and those double-headed blood axes, looking for booty, hard-earned cash. From every grand I made, the Vikings stole nine hundred. Now taxes aren't a problem for the truly rich. They're just to stop the have-nots getting wealthy. So we did what the Welsh had always done and took to the mountains, of Switzerland. Sybil and me and Gwen and Ifor set up our little Welsh Republic in the snow. A kind of Viking-free zone. From here we could spot a taxmen at a hundred paces, and they could read our lips – 'NO MORE TAXES!'

Jenks, it's time you and I had a serious chat. You're growing up and there are a few things you ought to know. I'm married, or hadn't you noticed? Her name's Sybil. I love her. You'd love her too. She's one of us, same blood, same side of the tracks. Her hair is silver. She's like a mother to me. But Jenks, I can't leave girls alone. She knows,

11

I think. She understands. Look, we're surrounded by limp-wrists in this game. It's no job for men, traipsing around in tights and make up. I'm not knocking them, some of my best friends are queens – really high camp royalty! But, 'Oh the women come and go, talking of Michelangelo.' I've steered a path through galaxies of stars, and starlets. If they were up and coming, so was I. In shrubberies, shower-rooms and in walk-in wardrobes – I came out once wearing the husband's suit! The question is, Jenks, why do I do it?

Now there are people called psychologists. They say obsessive womanising is symptomatic of latent homosexuality – yes, Jenks, one of those! It may be true, but if it is, isn't it uncomfortably close to the logic of O'Brien in Nineteen Eighteen-Four? Is freedom slavery? Is black just latent white? Was Einstein merely a latent subway mugger, you know, had a bad start in life, got into trouble with the laws of Physics? Psychologists complicate life. Perhaps people with inferiority complexes are just plainly inferior? Nothing complex! We have to believe in free will, we have no choice.

You're a lucky boy. We're both bloody lucky. And there's more than one brief shining moment on the road from Prince to King, to King... of Camelot!

Yes, the time was right for Camelot – an ancient legend sparkling with new hope, and I was living it. We all were. White House parties with the Kennedys. For one brief epoch, we walked in a new-found Kingdom of the Good. When I played the King again, twenty years on, I sensed that half the magic lay in the memories of audiences, looking back to that interlude of innocence, before the shots rang out in Dallas; before the clatter of helicopter blades above an alien jungle.

We all were courtiers in that dawn. I'd go back home, bearing messages from the Gods, and old schoolmates would say 'You've met him? You've met John Kennedy?' And I'd reply 'Why, yes. I shook hands with him, and Marlon Brando too.' And a voice chimed in from a corner of the bar, 'Watch that Brando, Richie! He could be a contender!'

Phone rings.

12

King Arthur speaking. Joseph Mankiewitz? Cleopatra? In Rome? With who?! How much? Plus villa and expenses? Talk to my agent. You'll have to buy me out of Camelot – never Welsh on a deal. It's called chivalry, love. Arrividerci!

What will be, shall be! Divinity, Adieu! Aye. There are those that Faustus most desires! Oh what a world of profit and delight, of power, of honour, of omnipotence is promised to the... movie star! Shall I make the spirits fetch me what I please?

Great Mephistopholes? One thing, good servant, let me crave of
thee. To glut the longing of my heart's desire,
That I may have unto my paramour
That heavenly Helen which I saw of late,
Whose sweet embraces may extinguish clear
Those thought that do dissuade me from my vow
And keep the vow I made to... Lucifer!

Oh, Marlowe bach!

I wonder what she'll be like, that vision from the poolside in Bel Air?

As to her person, it beggared all description: she did lie in her
pavilion – cloth-of-gold of tissue – o'er-picturing that Venus where
we see the fancy outwork nature. Age cannot whither her, nor
custom stale her infinite variety: other women cloy the appetites
they feed; but she makes hungry where most she satisfies: for vilest
things become themselves in her, that holy priests bless her when she
is riggish.

It took a long time, but at last she was talking to me.

Flashing bulbs, hubbub of press. Phone rings.

NO! This is Mark Antony's butler. He's busy right now – cunnilingus, you understand. It means an Irish air hostess!

Dials phone.

Front Desk? How much are they paying to put these phone calls through? Well I'll double it. Family and business only, got it?

Phone rings.

Don't you understand English? Oh! Philip! Sorry. No, I haven't been drinking. Yes, I got your wire. Philip. I know you're fond of Sybil, so am I. Listen Philip, I'm thirty-seven years old. Act like it? Now stop being an interfering old auntie. Philip! Philip! Damn! Says I've let him down. He's never let me down. Not ever. When I'm cast in a show, Philip's on the first plane out to coach me. Never missed.

Phone rings.

Ifor! Ifor, thank God. I've just had Philip on the line. Eddie Fisher's having a breakdown. Elizabeth's been rushed to hospital. Food poisoning supposedly. Sybil's upset? That's all you care about? But Ifor, don't hang up. Ifor... et tu Brute....

Dwi am briodi yr 'eneth 'ma... I will marry her....

Phone rings.

Jack! Jack, look, I know you're in charge of publicity but this is ridiculous. My fault? Jack, love, how was I to know she'd knock Krushchev off the front page? I know we're making a movie. Listen, love, why don't you just wind up Cleopatra and get the camera crews into my bedroom. Just me in my breastplate and Miss Tits. Much cheaper, and authentic. Well, it's cost three million already and art hasn't caught up with life yet. Elizabeth and I are way ahead of you. No we're not acting on set – it's for real. She wants to marry me. I'm married, that's why not! Yes, I have denied it. So I denied the denial. Should I deny that I denied the denial?

(Aside:) It's the most public adultery in the history of the world! Photographers, journalists, paparazzi!

I don't care if the Vatican does condemn the film, it's my life at stake here. No, no, no, divorce is out of the question. I've got two kids and Sybil. Yes, I love them all. So, your money's on Elizabeth. Bye Jack!

Phone rings.

Elizabeth? Elizabeth! I could tell. The ring of the telephone. Sounded different. Rwyn dy garu di! Mwy na neb arall yn y byd!

It means, *Sweet Helen, make me immortal with a kiss. Your lips suck forth my soul: see where it flies. Come, Helen, come, give me my soul again. Here I will dwell, for heaven is in those lips, and all is dross that is not Helena....*

Guess? It's Faustus. Marlowe. Chris Marlowe. Oh never mind! Look, I'll be right round. I've got to see you.

So. I've lost and won everything. I owe so much to Sybil and we're both so desperately worried about our little Jessica. She'll probably never speak. The doctors say a trauma. It doesn't add up. Me leaving now, just when the ties of blood are strongest. I keep thinking, thinking of that summer in Stratford, when the critics stamped my passport to good fortune. Sybil had given up acting for my career and to be mother to our children. Ten years we had to wait for them, ten years.

It's like leaving home at last. I owe everything to Syb and she'll have it – every single penny. Elizabeth will have to take me as I am, without a cent, and she's woman enough for that!

But, I have to be with Elizabeth. It's more potent than will, resolve or duty. Sometimes two people are like stars in each other's orbit. She blazes through my life like a daily Halley's comet, trailing sparks of celestial debris. You should see the bathroom. A massive fallout. Bras, slips, stockings, talc, perfume. The place is radioactive. She knows the world will go round picking things up after her. But she fusses over me. Brings me cooked lunch on set, makes me eat my greens, arranges my hair. Laughs at my stories. She's even drinking beer and watching rugby. Just wants to be the tidy wife. So it's love all right.

She's been called a 'chorus girl', a 'scarlet woman'. It can't be easy. And the Jenkins' of Pontrhydyfen. Their loyalties aren't easily transferred and we're a pretty overpowering clan. Well, wait till they hear I've stopped chasing, stopped wanting other women. Or rather, wait till they get around to believing it.

I'm on the monogamy wagon! In Camelot the chorus used to sing 'I wonder who the King is screwing tonight!' But now, I've met my match. Who is it she reminds me of? The eyes, the bearing and the presence. 'After this I say we will have no more marriages.'

And in the darkness of a thousand drab suburban cinemas, people pay to share our off-screen passion. We are the universal edition of every married partner's secret fling. A yearning that recedes before them like a half-remembered dream. And we get paid for it! Get married on the proceeds. After Cleopatra, some of the scripts we're sent are diabolical. My opinion of them is even lower than critics.

I mean the most incredible things happen in Hollywood, even before breakfast. Incredible. It's real-life cubism! In Hollywood they think Salvador Dali's just a lucky photographer. You know, just happened to be there when those watches were melting.

There was this guy, a producer – now, I swear to you this is true – and he knocked at my door one morning with two arms full of film from the cutting room floor. He says, 'I've just made this movie, and this stuff's left over. Seems a shame to waste it. Look!' And he ran it through his fingers against the light. It was all shots of army vehicles and personnel, in the desert, Second World War.

'Who's that?' I said.

He took the cigar from his mouth. 'George Peppard,' he said, 'but at a distance, it could be you.'

So we made this movie, oh, in a couple of weeks. He bought in some writers to write short scenes in between all those long shots from the trash bin. I played George Peppard in the close-ups and he played me long distance. Nobody knew. We put it on release and it did okay. Not big bucks, but it made money and I had fun doing it.

You know, when I was a kid I used to collect fresh horse and sheep dung and sell it to gardeners. Sixpence a bucket. Forty years later, it was selling for millions. How's that for inflation?

To salve my conscience I play Hamlet on Broadway. Johnny Gielgud makes me leading man. Hamlet, without women's clothing. Hamlet, American style – like a rehearsal. Hamlet, to standing ovations and rave notices. Hamlet, a record one hundred and thirty-six performances. A six million dollar Hamlet, a million of it mine.

Then, in Oxford, I really did sell out to the Devil. As Doctor Faustus. I knew that would please the literati. I fluffed my lines as Helen of Troy knocked back Bloody Marys in the wings. The Randolph Hotel never recovered from the shock. The critics enjoyed a week of vitriolic sadism; all the money went to charity and everybody had a wonderful time. The school prefects were vindicated. And Elizabeth and I shot off to Rome.

So here we are, the old story. Boy meets Girl. Just the two of us. And the secretaries. And the secretaries' secretaries, our private photographer, one valet each, a make-up artist, tutors for the kids, a governess, oh, and a nanny. Then there's the financial advisers, two accountants and a bodyguard. We even have to exercise the dogs on the roof in case they're dognapped – which would break Elizabeth's heart. And outside, in the corridor, there's a man with a machine-gun to stop anyone with another machine-gun bursting in to take us all prisoners. Yes, quite a large retinue really. We have to preserve our privacy even if it means sacrificing our privacy.

Bob? Where is he? Bob? Bob's my right hand man. Protects me from unwanted phone calls. If you want to contact anyone here, you have to put a message in a bottle and hope it finds dry land. Bob! I get a tidal wave of correspondence. What's this one. Good God, I remember him. We served in the RAF together. He was prop forward, I was flanker. Did we reply to this letter from Norfolk? Bob!

I wish I could just... walk out of here to a quiet bar across the street and have a chat – not a hope? Cleopatra fans everywhere screaming their bloody heads off. Thousands of them. We have to be spirited out of side doors, fire escapes, in laundry vans, police wagons. If I wanted to burgle this joint I'd know six different ways of getting in.

Picks up phone.

Engaged! It's always bloody engaged. Some force, some need, some thing elemental. As if a loss had been restored. I can't explain. She and I... it had to be.

Fade.

Optional interval.

ACT TWO

A rare privilege: my own obituaries. Rave notices? Not on your life. Even in death the critics descend on you. To judge the final performance. And I can tell you I'm destined for a poor exit.

The Times: 'Began his career as a performer of fine promise on the classical stage. This made it seem that he was destined for the commanding heights of the profession... in spite of occasional forays into the cin-e-ma.'

How now? Mend your speech a little, lest it may mar your fortunes!

'Virginia Woolf was powerful in purely cinematic terms.' Well, it was a bloody film!

'After 1947 he devoted himself to his stage career and to... the pursuit of young women who apparently found him irresistible.'

'Apparently!' An envious thrust, methinks, from one who lacks in penetration. Ah, listen to this. What does Johnny say... 'He was a born actor but he was a little bit wild and chose a rather mad way of throwing away his theatre career.' What an old... sweetie! 'He was cursed with enormous... sex appeal... he had only to turn those large blue eyes and every woman was smitten.'

When I do stare, see how the subject quakes! I pardon that man's life. What was thy cause? Adultery? Thou shalt not die! Die for adultery? No!

'Summoned by the Sirens of Hollywood.' 'A Prince who abdicated.' 'Immense promise not fulfilled.' 'In Sir John Gielgud's controversial production of Hamlet, Burton was... tensely exciting and moving...' – I say, steady on – 'but apparently visibly flawed.' Why 'apparently?' Quite simple. The chap who wrote this didn't see it. 'Visibly flawed' and he didn't even see it! Now there's perception for you!

The English critics can forgive you flouting convention. Hamlet in blue jeans. And they can understand rave notices. In America, the

Yanks are short on self control, long on razzmatazz. 'A mongrel breed.' A hundred and thirty-six performances on Broadway. You'll get away with that. But, to make a million as the Prince of Denmark... a million! Just not cricket old chap. Far more edifying to play Hamlet, in tights, in London, for peanuts, and submit yourself to ritual thrashings by The Times, the taxman and the master race. Then you can creep out of a lonely stage door, purged of arrogant pride, chastened by the literati, drown your sorrows in half a pint of bitter, and beg forgiveness from Art, from England, and from the Test and County Cricket Board. Flagellation – the English love it. They do it for the pain!

'The bastard Philip Faulconbridge in King John was a role he fitted exactly. He was the consummate bastard...', 'the most nominated actor never to win an Oscar.' 'Where did Burton go wrong? Perhaps nowhere....' Come on now, boys you're not trying. 'He never really came even close!' The Guardian: 'Burton colluded in the myth that he was a great actor.' The 'myth'?

They durst not do it. They could not, would not do it... tis worse than murder to do upon respect such violent outrage... how sharper than a serpent's tooth it is to have a thankless child.... Oh yes! I'm ready for Lear now!

(Sits, drinks.)

But not a Shakespeare audience. Have you ever looked at a Shakespeare audience? I don't want to be unkind, but have you? All those middle-aged ladies who regard it the way Catholics regard confession. A penance for not having sinned with real conviction. And they drag their golfing husbands along with them, and the poor fellows sit there horror-stricken, with eyes like liquorice allsorts. And it dawns on them that they did all this at school as a punishment, looking at their watches to see when the interval is due. Personally, I'd like to introduce positive vetting for Shakespeare audiences. Yes, the audience should be limited to, say two hundred who weren't frightened by Shakespeare in their cot.

Well I've blown the knighthood. Out of the window. Play Shakespeare in England – it has to be England, not Broadway – do it long enough, they make you one of the cast. A member of the court. But in the States it means nothing. Mind you, a lot of Americans do call me 'Sir Richard'. How very democratic, to be knighted by your fans. Even Philip Burton's been knighted over here. I really do believe that Americans are the most generous people on the Earth, enormously, extravagantly, funnily generous.

I was walking down Forty-Fifth Street in New York one day, and a little, powerfully built American guy stopped and embraced the whole sidewalk, the pavement, with his arms and said, 'Dick, God damn it, Dick, you are the greatest God-damn Macbeth the little woman and me have ever seen. You are the greatest God-damn Macbeth that ever lived!' And he went on and on telling me what a great Macbeth I was. Enormously generous. Surprising, as I've never actually played Macbeth. I think he might have seen me in... Henry the Fifth.

Whenever I play Shakespeare, no matter what the play, I'm awestruck by the depth of his understanding of the human soul. Can you imagine meeting, knowing, such a man? Still, I did get to know my countryman, Dylan Thomas, quite well.

One day, He and I were... having a drink. More than one drink, actually. Dylan never knew when to stop and I, I didn't want to. I recited some lines of the Scots poet, William Dunbar... 'Baith rich and poor of all degree. Timor Mortis Conturbat Me.' 'What do you think?' I asked him. There was a hushed silence. He slowly lit up a cigarette and replied, 'Wonderful stuff, marvellous! When did I write that?' 'Four hundred years ago – your Scotch period.' 'Four hundred years? Then it's about time I had another. Make it a double!' And we did. Many times over.

I'll tell you the real test of a sonnet. It's poetic even when delivered backwards.

Now, Bobby Kennedy loved poetry and he and I would have poetic contests in the White House. Wales versus Ireland at three paces. There was only one way to beat him – backward recitation of Shakespeare's Sonnet number thirty.

21

End sorrows and, restored are losses all,
Friend dear thee on think I....

Excuse me. I'm sorry. We all thought the world of him. I did the voice over for his campaign film when he ran for President. If we could only rewind on that one. I've acted tragedies, but a real one knocks you to the ground. Makes you realise... for most of our lives, we actors live a lie.

Ah well! What's a lie anyway? Isn't theatre just the noble art of deception? One glorious, enormous, hoodwinking lie. What does the God of Theatre care for the truth? Why, everything. Lies owe their very being to the truth. Somewhere in the bosom of a bawdy, brazen and Byzantine lie, there is the reason why it's told. Besides, lies are more interesting.

Now when the Welsh tell lies, we really mean it. What happened last week is unpredictable and today we invent yesterday. We must be true to our lie. Deliver it with passion; fashion its coils and let these colonise the galaxy of conscious being. There must be the lie, the whole lie, and nothing but the lie.

My old grandfather – now, this is the truth. He used to get about Pontrhydyfen by wheelchair, and Pontrhydyfen is hardly wheelchair country. It was Derby Day and Gran'f'thr had backed the winner – Black Sambo – so he thought he'd celebrate, get drunk. My father wheeled him down to the village pub, pulling on the chair to stop Gramps getting to the bar first. Vast quantities were sunk that night and – they left early – proceeding in good voice back up the hill, which had grown steeper with each pint. My father sees the front gate – no mean feat in his condition. And with simple, but defective, logic, lets go of the wheelchair to open it. He turns round. No grandfather. No indeed. Grandfather is halfway back to the pub at ever-gathering speed, backwards; receding to infinity. 'Come on Black Sambo! Come on Black Sambo! Come on boy....' At the bottom... was a solid, stone wall. You wouldn't have recognised him. Grandfather's winnings paid for his own funeral.

Light-years separated me from my father's underworld. You'd think that after losing grandfather, Dic Bach might have taken the pledge.

Never touched a drop. Not a bit of it. *I can recall him now, swaying in the doorway of our clean, bare kitchen. Looking with drunken benevolence at his large family. We'd all been warned by Ifor to look helpless, pitiful, reproachable, or downright bloody nasty. But the great smile, the black twinkling eyes, the unforgettable voice... were hard to resist. He'd slept out in a chicken coup – we could see the feathers in his hair. In his arms, he held a small, mangy, scrawny, emaciated greyhound, which he'd bought in the pub, and he proudly declared, 'Boys! Now all our troubles are over!'*

Some say social conditions drive a man to drink. Dic Bach did it because he liked it. Some of us do, you know.

When I was doing Beckett with Peter O'Toole, we stared unsteadily at each other. We knew that drastic measures were called for. We called the entire film crew together, and standing before them with two rattling china cups and saucers, pledged to drink nothing but tea for the entire shoot. It was an unconvincing ceremony. Then one of us blinked – and that was it! We were both scuba-diving in pure alcohol for one lost weekend. When King Peter had to put the ring on Chancellor Dickie's finger, it was like trying to thread a needle in boxing gloves.

I have an image in my mind. It is of a man perched on top of a wall. If he drops down on one side, he's made the last choice he will ever make. He denies himself all other options. He takes his place in an ordered, puritanical Utopia. No risks, no unforeseen eventualities.

On the other side, lies an uncertain world, where he is free to squander his talents or succeed, but most of all, to generally make a fool of himself. The man is poised on this wall not knowing which side to settle for. One side would be so mindbendingly, predictably dull it would surely drive him to drink. But in the wild excitement of the other, he'd freely choose to drink himself to death. Alec Leamass, bent on self-destruction, gripped by almost cosmic... boredom.

What the hell do you think spies are? Moral philosophers measuring everything they do against the word of God, or Karl Marx? Well, they're not. They're just a bunch of seedy, squalid bastards like me. Little men, drunkards, queers, hen-pecked husbands; civil servants playing cowboys and indians to brighten their rotten little lives. Do you think they sit like monks in London, balancing right against wrong? Yesterday, I'd have killed Mundt because I thought him evil and my enemy, but not today. Today he's evil and my friend. London needs him. They need him so that the great moronic masses that you admire so much can sleep soundly in their flea-bitten beds again; they need him for the safety of ordinary, crummy people like you and me....

After films like that it's nice to get back to Pontrhydyfen, and sanity. On one occasion I drove down there in my new Rolls. I met Sam the Drop. His aim in life was to be a public hangman. It was the first time I'd spotted Sam outside a pub during opening hours. He was admiring the Rolls and I asked him if he wanted a lift. He climbed into the back, sank into the upholstery, and began... testing the strength of the hand-strap with neck-snapping jerks. 'No', he said with a faraway look of nooses, hoods and trap doors, 'I'll just sit here and enjoy myself.'

Will Dai crossed over to us, hands in pockets, cap pulled well down. 'Well, if it isn't b... b... bloody D... D... Douglas... F... F... Fairbanks 'imself!' His stutter had always been bad.

'Hello Will. How are things, then?'

'T... T... Terrible m'n! I jus' l... l... lost s... s... seventy-f... five th... thousand p... p... pounds.'

'How come?'

'W... Well, I had s... s... seven draws on the f... f... football pools and j... jus' one team l... l... let me down....'

'Which team, Will?'

'Fuh... Fuh... Fuh...'

'Fulham?', I prompted him.

'No... no!'

'Falkirk!', I offered.

'N... n... no m'n, fuh... fuh... fuhkin' Swansea!'

Yes. It's nice to get back to sanity.

Ah Faustus, now hast thou but one bare hour to live and then thou must be damned perpetually. Stand still you ever moving stars of heaven, that time may cease and midnight never come.

In penthouse suites at the Dorchester I get up to watch the dawn coming up over London. Always first up. Elizabeth, the children, and the man with the machine-gun, all in dreamland. For me, dreaming is an effort these days. I can do whatever I like without anyone asking me what I'm doing or why. Ah. 'What infinite heart's ease must kings neglect that private men enjoy....' I've hired the most expensive floating dog kennel the world has ever seen. A thousand a week, to stop a chihuahua getting lonely in LA.

Oh lente, lente currite noctis equi. The stars move still, time runs, the clock will strike. The Devil will come and Faustus must be damned.

Let's drink to... the superfluous... the useless... the extravagant.

Diamonds for breakfast. Care to join us? Elizabeth beat me at ping-pong. Her Krupp's finest, thirty-three carat... five thousand bucks for every backhand volley. Ten thousand for a clean ace. Final score: one million – love. I wasn't playing my best. Slipping down the world's ping-pong ratings. It's Elizabeth they pay to see. Always notches up bigger earnings than I do. Let's drink to Venus de Milo. With or without ice?

The Devil will come and Faustus must be damned. Oh I'll leap up to my God! Who pulls me down? See, see where Christ's blood streams in the firmament; one drop would save my soul, half a drop. Ah, my Christ!

I've got a present. Now, this really is something. Her own private... ice rink. The Cartier diamond. Ari Onassis wanted this for Jacquie, but I outbid him. Sixty-nine point four-two per cent carat. I know she doesn't need it. But my God, I need to give it.

Oh, and these. The King of Spain once gave these very pearls to bloody Mary herself. (*Puts pearls on head.*) 'Oh I know a bank where the wild thyme blows...' and a yacht with a pool and a cocktail lounge and an organ as big as an oil refinery.... We can hire an organist to play Bach when there's a storm at sea. Tocatta and Fugue in sea minor.

And see where God stretcheth out his arm and bends his ireful brows. Mountains and hills, come and fall on me, and hide me from the heavy wrath of God.

(*Facing the back curtain.*)

Where the hell is everybody? All these gems of the poetic imagination going to waste. I need an audience!

(*Turns to face audience.*)

You stars that reigned at my nativity,
Whose influence hath allotted death and hell,
Now draw up Faustus like a foggy mist
Into the entrails of yon labouring cloud
That when you vomit forth into the air
My limbs may issue from your smoky mouths,
So that my soul may but ascend to heaven.

Know what we'll ascend to heaven on? Our own fur-lined twin engine jet. Each day it gets harder and harder to scale new heights of vulgarity. All our Van Goghs, Monets, Modiglianis. They offend my social... socialist sensib... sensibilities. Elizabeth was born to this. She can cope. Van Gogh, Monet, Modigliani – artists of integrity. I mean, you'd never catch Van Gogh playing the lead in 'Where Eagles Dare' now would you? Makes a bad impression. Mind you, he'd have given his left ear for that kind of fee.... 'This is Vincent calling Danny Boy... Vincent calling Danny Boy.' Why do you think I give so much of it away?

Elizabeth's worried that her arms are getting fat. Know what I say?

If thine right arm offend thee, knock it off. That's what Venus de Milo did. Oh! One day I'm going to turn my back on all this. I'm going to be an... honorar... an honorary fellow, Oxford University. At St Peter's. Dreaming spires. A don, giving classes in literature....

Impose some end to my incessant pain. Let Faustus live in hell a thousand years. A hundred thousand, and at last be saved. Oh, no end is limited to damned souls. Why... wert thou not a creature wanting soul?

Last night, Elizabeth broke a whole service of dinner plates over my head. Was it something I said? We each create the partner we deserve. Not many people know that.

Oh why is this immortal that thou hast... ah, Pythagoras metempsychosis, were that true. This soul should fly from me and I be changed unto some brutish beast....

How's the rest of it go?

All beasts are happy, for when they die their souls are soon dissolved into elements... but mine must live and still be plagued in hell.

Hell? It's her birthday! We'll fly in five square feet of caviar, fill the bath with Moet and Chandon 1923 and you can all dive in naked. Come on in! It's lovely once you're in! I've invited the Royal family. They can tell us jokes....

Oh Jesus, I feel awful. What's the matter with me?

(Falls flat on back.)

Look not... so fierce on me... adders, serpents, let me breathe awhile... and....

(Pause.)

Haven't you realised, I've dried, gone up, forgotten my lines. Just like I did at Oxford.

(*Leans up on elbow.*)

I keep ribbing Elizabeth that she's never learnt anything by heart. She said it's not true. So I say, come on then you fat Jewish tart, let's hear it. And she goes....

'What'll you have?', the waiter said, as he stood there picking his nose. Two hard boiled eggs, you son of a bitch, you can't stick your fingers in those!' Richard's himself again!

Let's see now, what else can we do? There are other games we can play. We've played 'Humiliate the Host'. We've gone through the one... how about, how about 'Hump the Hostess'? How about that. Or shall we save that one for later? You know, mount her like a god-damn dog! Oh, you don't want to play 'Hump the Hostess' you don't want to play that one. Not yet. I know what we'll play, we'll play 'Get the Guests!' How about a little game of 'Get the Guests'?

Who is afraid Virginia Woolf?

Are we, Richard and Elizabeth, playing George and Martha? Or are we – my God, can it be – are we, George and Martha, playing Richard and Elizabeth? The lines remember me; the play interprets us. Well, you know, nothing can survive a play about itself. Actors cannot act themselves. It's like imitating reflections in a mirror, impersonating shadows.

It's hard to tell you this Martha. I mean, Elizabeth. While you were out, making your last movie, the doorbell rang. It was a telegram. From Mr Albee. It was for us. I can hardly bring myself to say it. I'm afraid our marriage won't be coming to it's own anniversary party. No. Our marriage can't make it that day. You see, it had been drinking rather heavily, and wrapped itself round a tree whilst trying to avoid middle age. So it's Goodbye Elizabeth, at least, for now. Oh God....

I play Richard! You hear me, father! I play Richard. I wear the crown. The crown is mine! I'm drunk like you! Is the madness in me too? Oh God, is the taint in me too, father!

God I feel awful. What's the matter with me? Look I, I'm shaking. I'm pouring with sweat. Can it be, can it be that, after forty-eight years, I'm finally having a hangover? How many did I have? My usual – three. My head's spinning. Three bottles? Never made me feel like this before. Must be the cigarettes. I must cut down. To fifty. Oh, this is intolerable. I'm not putting up with it! Those stupid doctors at St John's....

Two weeks they've given me, two weeks. Look, it's not that I'm afraid of death – I just can't be killed off this easily. I'm from Welsh mining stock. They promised to come to my funeral. Two weeks drinking time left? Ding-ding, Last call. They say they don't think they can save me even if I stop right now. Doctors love to play God. Damn them!

I dreamed there was an Emperor Antony: O such another sleep that I might see but such another man! His face was as the heavens; and therein stuck a sun and moon, which kept their course and lighted the little O, the Earth... think you there was, or might be, such a man as this I dreamed of?

Hello... get me St John's Clinic, Santa Monica... it's urgent... thank you.

Four days off drink. It was bad. Very bad. Always the same. I would dream of my brother Ifor who'd died four years earlier. Ifor was a father to me. Kind, gentle, strong. Never spared me frankness. I would dream he was with me in the room....

It was Autumn of 1968 the... accident happened. I suddenly had this urge to take my daughter Kate to Switzerland to see her first home – 'Pays de Galles'. We had taken Kate to lunch, and – as I had settled in for afternoon cocktails – Ifor went on ahead to heat the place. By the time I got round to coffee, two hours had passed. When we finally got up to the house, it was a... nightmare. Ifor was lying in the snow. His neck was broken. He was barely alive. He'd been there two whole hours. Slipped on a snow-grill. I tried... I tried... to lift him. Shouldn't have. Damn drink....

We got him to Geneva. Intensive care. Gwen and Elizabeth flew straight out.

At sixty-one, Ifor was paralysed from the neck down.

There were moments when he didn't want to live and, sometimes, after visiting him or Jessica, I felt the same. *His life was gentle, and the elements so mixed in him that Nature might stand up and say to all the world this was a man!*

I got back to work. That was something. Playing Churchill. Well, if an Irishman called Harris can play Cromwell, I'm pretty sure a Welsh miner can manage Churchill. I was doing 'Hamlet' once, at the Old Vic. I had just begun the performance, when I became aware of a deep rumbling from the front row of the stalls! Well, It was Churchill. Reciting the lines with me. And I could not shake him off – I tried going faster, I tried going slower. We made cuts. And each time I made a cut – a small explosion occurred! Now, the old man was notorious for not staying throughout a performance if he disapproved, so in the interval I looked through the peephole in the curtain. I'd lost him! Back at my dressing room there was a knock on the door, and there stood Churchill. He gave a deep bow, like the great Elizabethan courtier he was, and said, 'My Lord Hamlet, may I use your bathroom?'

But as I played Churchill, I recalled stories about him sending troops in 1910 against the miners. I wrote something to that effect in a newspaper and all bloody hell broke loose. Apparently, it wasn't true. Lifelong friends turned their backs on me. I was slated in The Times. Some... man, called Norman Tebbit, was particularly nasty. Churchill always liked my work. We'd never clashed on a personal level. All the same, the old man deserved my respect. In 1940, he stood alone against a barbarous Europe. On a bottle of brandy a day.

Yes, a difficult time really. All the heroes of my life dying around me. The doctors warning me I could be next. And so, the inevitable happened. One day, Elizabeth and I found ourselves on two ends of the same telephone line, and the temptation to meet up again was irresistible.

I think it was Karl Marx who said 'History repeats itself... but the second time as farce.' And so, on the banks of a muddy river in Botswana, we were married for the second time, watched by one bewildered Hippopotamus. It was to be 'for lovely always' and 'lovely always' lasted seven weeks.

Of course I was back on this stuff. On and off....

(*Empties vodka bottle.*)

But you can't kick two habits at once; and I confess to a chronic 'beautiful woman' addiction.

I'd just met Susan on the ski-slopes of Gstaad,
swirling earthbound in a halo of frozen sunlight;
Her smile could put an avalanche into reverse gear.
Susan – my saviour, delivered me from
late-Elizabethan vodka bottles, dog-ends
and the acrid smell of matrimonial blitzkreig.
Susan put me on the stage again – my Equus was a galloping success.
Broadway stomped its feet for no-good boyo and his phantom horse.

Susan – seven years of achievement and serenity –
But the role of Burton's wife is far from easy
like riding side-car on the wall of death,
a woman can only take so much
'Yet each man kills the thing he loves...'
Oh Oscar! You put your finger on it, boy!
You put your finger on it!

We were making 'Wagner'. I was making Wagner. During the seven months of filming, I began to look like Wagner, behave like Wagner. From the start of my Gotterdammerung, Susan lasted just four weeks.

It was then that one of the most shameful events of my life occurred. I took a drink. In fact, I... I suddenly hit it very hard. Three 'knights' later – Sir Larry, Sir John, Sir Ralph – they were flown out to join us for the filming. I've always believed that once a king always a king, but... once a knight's enough.

I'd already had a row with some Italian cameraman. I told him

Mickey Mouse had better camera angles and he was giving me all this intellectual crap about the spiritual meaning of light and shade, which, of course, I know everything about. I'm colour blind. And that night at dinner I reminded Olivier that he'd once called me 'second-rate'. Of course he denied it. He came on with 'But dear boy, we all know you're the greatest actor in the world.' A real put down.

'You call me second-rate? You know the part you're playing in this film? You're playing a second-class minister, a second-class chief of police.... It's a second-class role. I am Wagner. I am the star. The tables are turned.'

Why the hell did I do that?

We're making a film here.

Nineteen Eighty-Four. The year I've been rehearsing for. My last! The part! It used to be fifty-eight takes and fifty-eight vodkas, but not now. Now... I'm dry.

They've said I can use... the 'Richard Burton' voice. How kind. I've been waiting to... do a Burton. I like playing Burton. It's the greatest role Ritchie Jenkins ever got to play! Paul Schofield broke a leg. I've told him he should often enough. So I get to play... that evil swine from the Ministry of Truth. O'Brien doesn't even get pleasure out of torture.

Do not imagine you will save yourself, Winston, however completely you surrender to us. No one who has once gone astray is ever spared. And even if we chose to let you live out of the natural term of your life, still you would never escape us. What happens to you here is forever. Understand that in advance. We shall crush you down to the point from which there is no coming back. Things will happen to you from which you could never recover if you lived a thousand years. Never again will you be capable of love, or friendship, or joy of living, laughter, or curiosity, or courage, or integrity. You will be hollow. We shall squeeze you empty. And then we shall fill you with ourselves.

Could it be possible, I wonder, ever to do that? Completely drain a man of his identity and create a totally new one? Well, actors try. But how much of you survives?

(*He turns to the chair.*)

Jenks! There's a lot of unemployment in these parts. Bad news, boyo! I'm offering you a job. No, not mining – mining is the pits, I know. There's a lot of money in it... a couple of million. There, there lovely boy, I know its hard to bear. You'll have to sleep with the world's most beautiful women. Don't fret, there's worse to come. You'll play the Prince the way no Prince could dream of; your Kings will not be bettered by the best; you'll make the silence speak, the stillness move; you'll teach the English how to speak their lovely language. And all this, Jenks, shall be deemed an 'abdication', 'falling short', an 'unfulfilled ambition, unrealised potential!' You'll 'never even come close!' He says it's better than the haberdashery! Good boy! I knew I could count on you.

(*Spotlight from front, on Burton's face.*)

And now, as I am ready to come to terms with it all, finally to take possession of the essential core of my being, right now I am aware of the presence of a stranger. He comes uninvited to my threshold, quite by chance, to deny me in that same spirit in which the gift was granted. Without passion, without purpose, without drama. His sense of timing is sublime, artless.

Gradually I was aware of someone in the doorway and turned my eyes that way and saw, carved out of the sunlight, a man who stood watching me... so still, there was not other such stillness anywhere on the earth... so... still... that the air seemed to leap at his side. He came towards me and the sun flooded its banks and flowed across the shadow. He asked me why I stood alone. His voice hovered on memory with open wings and drew itself up from a chime of silence, as though it had long time lain in a vein of gold.

'Tomorrow and tomorrow and tomorrow....'

'Our revels now are ended.'

The End.

BIRTHMARKS

The main political and personal incidents dramatised in this play are true in fact and chronology. The rest is true in substance. The only unsubstantiated elements are Konrad's innocent romance and the involvement of Mr Rabin. All viewpoints, however controversial, and the language in which they are expressed, are drawn largely from the personal correspondence and writings of the real-life characters.

> *'What is the secular basis of Judaism? Practical need, self interest. We recognise in Judaism therefore, a general anti-social element of our time. Contempt for theory, art, history and for man as an end in himself.... Once society has succeeded in abolishing the empirical essence of Judaism – Huckstering and its preconditions, the Jew will have become impossible.'*
>
> Karl Marx, 'On the Jewish Question', 1844.

> *'As to the carbuncles, here is how things stand. Today I took a razor to the swine on my groin. The putrid blood spurted up high....'*
>
> Karl Marx, Marx – Engels Correspondence editor Fritz Raddatz.

> *'We must re-fuck the Communist Manifesto!'*
>
> Karl Marx, Marx – Engels Correspondence editor Fritz Raddatz.

Original Cast

Karl Marx, aged 32 - Laurence Llewellyn
Frederick Engels, aged 30 - Ian May
Jenny Marx, aged 37 - Alison Jenkins
Helen (Lenchen) Demuth,
aged 27 - Clêr Stephens
Mr Rabin (landlord), aged 65 } John Atkinson
August Willich, aged 40
Konrad Schramm, aged 26 } Nick Bowman
Doctor, aged 65

Director - Jeremy James

ACT ONE
Scene One – Home from Home

Late autumn, 1849, Soho, London. A dimly lit, bare room with door, backstage right; a mantelpiece and fireplace, centre; a small window, left side.

MR RABIN is an old Jewish cockney, but the Jewishness should not be overplayed. ENGELS is a young man, fair haired, handsome and well dressed with hat and cane. They have just come upstairs to view an empty flat, which ENGELS wants to rent for the Marx family. The older man is out of breath. ENGELS wanders around, inspecting.

RABIN: This friend of yours, Mr...?

ENGELS (*misconstruing*): Engels. Herr Engels.

RABIN: No. The dark gentleman, yesterday.

ENGELS: Mohr.

RABIN (*nods*): Mr Mohr.

ENGELS: I'm standing in for him.

RABIN: Jewish name?

ENGELS: His family... used to be.

RABIN: 'Used to be?'

ENGELS: He can't make it today. (*Looks around.*) Too busy!

RABIN (*waves his arm around the flat*): But how will he know if it suits him?

ENGELS (*investigating each corner*): He says it's not important.

RABIN: Not important? A home?

ENGELS: He trusts my judgement.

RABIN (*shrugs*): Well, this is it!

ENGELS: 'It?'

RABIN: Finest flat in Soho! This flat has everything. Walls! (*Smooths a wall with his hand.*) Look: floor! (*Stamps foot lightly.*)

ENGELS (*stamps foot hard*): Floor!

RABIN: Not too hard! Everything!

ENGELS: Everything?

RABIN (*walks up close to ENGELS*): Roof also! (*Points upwards.*)

ENGELS (*looking up*): Ah! Roof!

RABIN: And also 'extras.'

ENGELS: 'Extras?'

RABIN: You want extras. Here, look. (*Points.*) Door! The one we came through. Some door, that!

ENGELS: You've thought of everything.

RABIN: You get out of this room by the same door.

ENGELS: So versatile!

RABIN: It's luxury, I tell you. Such a flat! (*Walks to window.*) There! Windows, too!

ENGELS (*following*): But, you can't see through it.

RABIN: Of course! (*Rubs circle with cuff-sleeve.*) There! (*Puts on specs.*) Crystal clear!

ENGELS: Does it open?

RABIN: Does it open! Does it open! (*Struggles with window.*) It doesn't open.

ENGELS (*opens it with ease, noise of street vendors, horses, carts, etc., pulls away from stench*): Eergh!

RABIN: Opens perfectly.

ENGELS: The stench!

RABIN: For the smell, I don't charge.

ENGELS: What about the neighbours?

RABIN: Upstairs – Italians. Downstairs – my shop.

ENGELS: Italians? Do they sing?

RABIN: They got nothing to sing about! (*Confidentially.*) Eight kids! What about your friend?

ENGELS: Er?

RABIN: Have you lost count?

ENGELS (*counts on fingers*): He's got... three.

RABIN: You don't seem sure.

ENGELS: And a half.

RABIN: Two rooms should be enough for six of them.

ENGELS: Seven.

RABIN: Four kids, plus him and his wife: six.

ENGELS: And his housekeeper.

RABIN: Housekeeper! That I should have a lodger with a housekeeper! What did I say the rent was?

ENGELS (*sighs wearily, turns to leave*): You said twelve shillings and six pence a week. That's already too much.

RABIN: Wait! Wait! (*ENGELS halts.*) Your friend's Jewish? (*More of a statement than a question.*)

ENGELS: What's this? An interrogation?

RABIN: A landlord should know his tenant.

ENGELS: And a tenant his landlord?

RABIN: Do I live in his house? (*Pause.*) What's he do, this friend of yours? His occupation.

ENGELS (*circumspect yet thoughtful*): His profession is the Welfare of Man.

RABIN (*nods world wearily*): Keeps him busy, does it?

ENGELS: Well, he also writes, as I do.

RABIN: About?

ENGELS (*reluctantly*): Politics.

RABIN (*concerned*): Politics! You're not mixed up in politics?

ENGELS: Not exactly.

RABIN: Then what?

ENGELS: We write about revolution, to be precise.

RABIN (*relieved*): Oh! You had me worried for a minute! (*They smile.*) I thought you meant real politics!

ENGELS (*laughs to cover up*): Good heavens, no!

RABIN: Writing! A nice quiet occupation. But if I might make a suggestion.

ENGELS: Please do.

RABIN: You write about revolution. Let others do it. Safer!

ENGELS: Only they can do it. Only they!

RABIN: Exactly. And – you don't mind do you? – this writing business. (*Whispers.*) Tell your friend to get into publishing. Get someone else to do the writing.

ENGELS: Business? Where's the worth in that? (*In deep thought, somewhat unaware of RABIN.*) My friend would say that working for the world uplifts a man.

RABIN (*trying to snap him out of it*): Work for your wife and kids. That's hard enough!

ENGELS (*composed*): Imparts nobility to all his deeds, makes him invulnerable!

RABIN: Oh my Gawd! A Rabbi!

ENGELS: Mohr doesn't believe in any of that.

RABIN: Not believe? Ah! An academic! (*Pauses, cagily.*) Mmmh I've seen his face before. (*Trying to recall.*) A painting! (*Snaps fingers.*) Rabbi Jehuda!

ENGELS: Who-da?

RABIN: Of Padua. Italy. Fifteenth century.

ENGELS: That would make Mohr, say, four hundred years old.

RABIN: So. He's got a young face!

ENGELS: He's not Italian.

RABIN: What are we, any of us? (*Wanders to window.*) Look down there: Germans, Italians, Chinamen and Poles. To them, England is home.

ENGELS: It's exile.

RABIN (*chuckles, points to window*): They came to England because in their own lands they were already exiles!

ENGELS: Well. Spare me the philosophy.

RABIN: Philosophy! (*With a twinkle.*) Above my head, I'm afraid but what do you think of twelve bob a week?

ENGELS (*considering*): The Museum Library is close at hand.

RABIN: All free.

ENGELS: Outside the German Hotel in Leicester Square are a homeless wife and some very tired children.

RABIN (*wearily*): All right. So, eleven shillings.

ENGELS: That's the idea.

RABIN: It's a deal.

ENGELS: When can they move in?

RABIN: Tonight. Tell you what – boy next door, I'll give him six pence to help with the furniture.

ENGELS: They have very little furniture.

RABIN: So I'll give him threepence.

They walk to the door. RABIN halts.

RABIN: To change the world. It could take ages, so the rent is in advance.

Fade.

Scene Two – Love

LENCHEN at the window, whispering loudly to KONRAD SCHRAMM in the street below. LENCHEN is an earthy, witty, no-nonsense girl, whose egalitarian approach to life is evident in her relations with others. She is also sexually provocative when she wishes to be.

SCHRAMM (*voice off*): Tonight then?

LENCHEN: Can't Konrad. Too busy!

SCHRAMM (*voice off*): Just one drink in the Tavern?

LENCHEN: Any food?

SCHRAMM (*voice off as he falls over a dustbin*): Aaah!

LENCHEN (*laughs*): You're accident prone. All right?

SCHRAMM: I'm covered in garbage. Ach!

Closes window as JENNY enters. JENNY is well-bred, confident, cultured, but without any haughtiness or arrogance of her status as the daughter of a baron. She leaves the heavier tasks to LENCHEN, mainly because she is an overworked mother. She is reading from an old letter she has found.

JENNY: Listen to this. Here's an old one, found it sorting through the trunk. (*She reads it, laughing coyly at her past words.*) 'Dear Karl, I dreamed that you had been wounded in a duel on my behalf...'

LENCHEN: A Jew with a sword! I can't cope with it!

JENNY: Sshhhh! 'And Karl, I was in a state of rapture and of bliss because of that...'

LENCHEN: You were in a bad way!

JENNY (*sniggers*): 'You see sweetheart, I thought I could now become quite indispensable to you...' I can't go on!

LENCHEN walks across. Snatches the letter. Walks away reading it.

JENNY (*still laughing, chasing after her*): No, Lenchen, no!

LENCHEN (*over her shoulder with gentle mockery*): 'You would then always keep me with you and love me (*puts tongue in cheek*) and I could write down all your heavenly ideas and be really useful to you. Love Jenny.' (*Playfully.*) Ah, Sweet!

JENNY: And here we are – Romantic Soho! Help me with the trunk! (*They slide a trunk in from just inside a back bedroom door and pause for breath, blowing.*)

LENCHEN: Here Jen! I've worked it out.

JENNY: What?

LENCHEN: The square root of 'bellyache squared'. It's bellyache!

JENNY: Mnnh! 'The mathematics of hunger.'

LENCHEN: Can't Charley touch the General for a few quid? Or tell him to put a sausage in the post?

JENNY: Herr Engels has promised five pounds. I know he can afford it, but I hate accepting it.

LENCHEN: Thank God for capitalists! Or we communists would starve!

JENNY: I had to sell the beds. Creditors!

LENCHEN: Well, flog the table. We only eat off it.

JENNY: What's Mohr going to write on?

LENCHEN: Never mind! At Uncle's they reckon one in three croaks in Soho. I could be the lucky one.

JENNY: 'Croaks?'

LENCHEN (*'slits' throat with forefinger*): Lllch! Cholera! Can't you whiff the sewers?

JENNY: What's all this cockney talk? Who's Uncle?

LENCHEN: The Pawnshop! (*Affectation.*) Now would 'Modom' care to show one to one's room?

JENNY: It'll have to be (*points downstage left*) that corner.

LENCHEN lobs her bundle into the corner.

JENNY (*walks to bedroom door*): Come on! Roll call!

LENCHEN peers inside.

JENNY: How is the Empress of China?

LENCHEN: Sleeping with her eyes open.

JENNY: Hottentot?

LENCHEN: Blacked out!

JENNY: Edgar?

LENCHEN: Out like a light!

JENNY (*with some concern*): And little Guido?

LENCHEN: Dead to the world. (*Stops herself.*) Well, restless.

JENNY: He's hungry. But my breasts are cracked and sore. He's taking blood in with the milk.

LENCHEN: You're tired, Jen, it's all the moving. Come on. Let's do the shrine.

They move to place trinkets on the mantelpiece.

JENNY (*her spirits lifting again*): Pass the silver! And the silver spoons.

LENCHEN passes two items and spoons and JENNY arranges them fondly on the mantel.

LENCHEN: I know! Flog these and get your knickers out of hock!

JENNY: No. The silver is a gift from Grandmama.

LENCHEN: What's this crest on 'em?

JENNY: The Duke of Argyll, a distant cousin. (*Claps hands.*) Come! The damask!

LENCHEN passes the damask napkins and JENNY arranges them. It is in sharp contrast to the dire poverty all around them.

JENNY: There. Doesn't it look splendid!

LENCHEN (*shakes head smiling*): Look at you! Hardly any shoes on your feet, yet you keep these trinkets.

JENNY: It reminds me of a time when money didn't matter.

LENCHEN: It'll change. You see. As soon as Charley's got this Economics shit out of his system.

JENNY: Lenchen!

LENCHEN: His words. Not mine. (*Imitating Marx loudly.*) 'Economic Shit!'

JENNY: Charming! You know, Mohr really does hate money. It's a physical aversion. On honeymoon Mama gave us a strongbox, a little chest.

LENCHEN: The one we hocked to pay the bookseller?

JENNY: Yes, that one, and it was full of gold coin, silver, notes. He left the chest on the table and any guest who came to call was told 'Here! Take! Help yourself!'

LENCHEN: Don't. It makes me ill. It's unnatural!

JENNY: Money is Mohr's malady. Thinking of it gives him migraine. Writing of it turns his blood, and yet, he must.

LENCHEN: An 'article' that grew into a pamphlet. Now its 'Volume One'.

JENNY: It's taken out a mortgage on his life. (*With concern.*) He'll never finish it.

LENCHEN: He will. Give him a year, and then.... (*Throws up her arms.*) They'll recognise him as a genius. Make him Professor at Oxford University or something.

JENNY: You believe in him as much as I do.

LENCHEN: He's bloody great, our Charley! Brilliant!

JENNY: You're good to him. To all of us.

LENCHEN: I only do it for the money!

JENNY: This life in exile. Where's it leading? Intrigues. Petty jealousies. Backbiting! Hmh! The Party. Some comrades!

LENCHEN: There's no child without birth pangs. You should know.

JENNY: So. We're the midwives to this 'child'?

LENCHEN: Aye... and this one's a right little terror!

Fade.

Scene Three – Arsebuncles

Late evening. LENCHEN is asleep with her head on the table. JENNY emerges stretching from the bedroom. She yawns. Nudges LENCHEN.

MARX (*voice off as door slams outside*): Jenny! Jenny!

LENCHEN: Hark! The conquering hero comes!

MARX (*enters, stops, holds temples with ten fingers*): My head is bursting. Lenchen!

LENCHEN: Tea, your Lordship? I can read your thoughts. (*Pours tea.*)

MARX: It's a real swine, this headache! A real German one! A skull-splitter. There's something the matter with my grey matter. It's about to spew forth.

JENNY: You should have slept last night instead of reading.

MARX (*holding forehead*): Don't start now. Have some sympathy for an ailing cranium!

LENCHEN: There! A cup o' sympathy. (*She exits.*)

JENNY: Komm! Komm mal her! Sit down. Relax a moment! (*Prepares a chair.*)

MARX (*sits and jumps up*): Aaaargh!!!

JENNY: What is it?

MARX: Another boil! On the bum! I'd forgotten about it walking home. It's like Vesuvius! I'm exploding at both ends. Is it

48

brainboxbuncle or a simple arse-ache? Some demon is inside me trying to get out!

JENNY (*quietly*): Stop fussing. Undo your trousers!

MARX does so. He faces audience at an angle. She pulls his trousers down from the front.

JENNY: Now! Let's have a close look!

She goes around to the back of MARX. Crouches and peers closely at an angle to audience.

MARX: Promise not to lance it!

He wheels round bum to rear of stage. She follows.

JENNY: I'm not your Lady Lancelot.

MARX: See anything? Was machst du?

JENNY: Keep still! It's dark down here.

LENCHEN (*enters on some errand, folds arms*): I do love these tender moments, don't you?

MARX: Get out Lenchen, can't you.

LENCHEN: Listen Charley, I've seen more big babies' bums than we've had hot dinners and I mean that literally!

MARX: A man's arse is private property.

LENCHEN (*comes closer to look*): I see now who Laura takes after. Spitting image.

MARX: Thank you. Take the rest of the day off.

JENNY trying to suppress laughter with LENCHEN, and holding her mouth.

LENCHEN: If the Prussian police could see you now! Hold it! I'll get a photographer. (*Exits.*)

MARX (*peers round*): Was ist? Garfunkel?

JENNY: Nein! Furunkel! Eine grosse Arschfurunkel!

MARX: Brilliant! If it spreads to my Schwantz, our love-life's kaput.

JENNY: A change is as good as a rest!

She mixes hot water in a bowl and tears an old sheet.

MARX: That's all I need! Carbuncular furuncular eruptions. I'll have to write standing up. Don't squeeze it! I'm very attached to this boil. I've been working on it for days.

JENNY: A poultice will draw out the puss.

MARX: It's not hot, is it?

JENNY: Not really. (*Slaps it on.*)

MARX: Ow! Do you think the romance has gone out of our marriage?

JENNY: 'Romance?' What's that? There. Hold this cloth over it. Now! I'll pull up your pants. Sit down, gently.

LENCHEN (*voice off*): I'm going out for an hour – just the tavern.

JENNY: All right.

MARX: Oh! Oh relief at last. S'funny, my headache's gone.

JENNY (*kisses his forehead*): Lenchen's right. You need regular sleep and a good relaxing bath.

MARX: One bum poultice – headache completely gone! (*Lights up clay pipe.*)

JENNY: And you shouldn't smoke so much.

MARX: Any sign of Flash Ikey?

JENNY: Mr Rabin?

MARX: Stopped me in the street for the rent, wanted to know had I started a business yet! Business! Schmizness!

JENNY: Yes, he did call up. We're three weeks overdue with the rent!

MARX (*grimacing, grasping, mocking*): Alberich, so ein bleiner rutschiger Typ!

JENNY: And Karl, one of the silver plates is missing.

MARX: I know. I sent Lenchen to pop it to Uncle's yesterday.

JENNY: Mohr, I wish you'd discuss it with me first. It's not fair on her.

MARX: Do you know how much they advanced on it? Four pounds! No wonder they've got three balls hanging up outside – two of them are mine!

JENNY: You must not place her in a position where she has to deceive me, it comes between us.

MARX: So! I promise!

JENNY: So where's the four pounds?

MARX: The wine merchant insisted.

JENNY: Never mind the wine merchant, what about the baker?

MARX: I paid him too.

JENNY: And the money for the ironmonger, the greengrocer and the rest?

MARX (*tired*): Here, take this. (*Offers notes hastily to get them out of his hands.*)

JENNY: Mohr, Twenty pounds! Where did you get this?

MARX: Take it. Get the plate back from Uncle.

JENNY: Karl are you sure?

MARX: I'm sure my love, take it. Dreckiges Jüdisches Geld! Aaach, I hate it. I feel dirty when I hold it in my hands.

JENNY: It seems to hate you too my sweetheart, all of us. (*Sits on floor at his knees.*)

MARX: It's a thin veil of slime and scum which gets into people's eyes and blinds them to all things truly human. Scheisse!

JENNY caresses his knee and kisses it. MARX stands up abruptly and walks around.

MARX: I wish my mother would cough up with that inheritance. She's just sitting on it, accumulating interest, like a boil. Where's the sense in it? It's in the blood you see, while we're scrabbling around for crusts.

JENNY (*smiling*): I was copying out your notes this morning.

MARX: Which ones?

JENNY: On Malthus's theory of rent.

MARX (*amused*): Oh that! What a prize fart Malthus is! In a roomful of mediocrities, he'd stand head and shoulders below the rest. Pigmy! He couldn't even piss straight!

JENNY: And it occurred to me how funny it was.

MARX: Malthus? Funny?

JENNY: No! That I was writing out all this stuff on the declining rentability of land, and...

MARX (*seeing the joke*): And our rent was going up! (*Laughs aloud.*)

JENNY (*getting hysterical*): And we hadn't paid it! And your mother, bless her heart, says...

MARX (*putting on heavy German accent*): 'Karl, always you are writing about capital, never you are making any already!' (*More laughter. Snaps fingers.*) Here! Good news... (*Feels in pocket. Produces a card.*)

JENNY: Mohr, you've got it! At last.

MARX: My own desk! My own seat at the British Museum.

JENNY: Wonderful!

MARX: Now I can start!

JENNY: Start?

MARX: Yes. All these notes are just the beginning. This boil is just the beginning. You know I find one reference just leads me to another, then another and I begin to establish a whole galaxy of interconnections. I can't begin to write until I know it all. All. Until I have internalised all that is external. Recreated it all up here. (*Taps head quietly.*) Only then am I in control and then I feel as though it's accumulating inside me, turning into something strangely terrible and new.

JENNY: And then you stay up all night!

MARX: It's the only time there's any peace in here. Hier ist es wie im Irrenhaus!

She embraces him and he kisses her forehead.

MARX: It's only you who keeps me sane, and the dictatorship of

53

Lenchen. By the way, there's a meeting here Thursday week.

JENNY: Oh no! Why here?

MARX: The tavern's too expensive. It's only the Committee.

JENNY: But what about the children and...

MARX (*firmly staving off criticism*): It'll be short, very short. Possibly the last! (*Briskly.*) Now. Leave me! I must work.

He walks towards table. JENNY heads for door. His mood suddenly changes as he lifts up items looking for something. He becomes extremely tense because his desk has been tampered with.

MARX: Where's that book! Who's been moving my things?

JENNY: Sorry, my love?

MARX: Owen! 'The Revolution in Mind and Practice.'

JENNY (*getting anxious*): What colour is it?

MARX: Why do people touch my things? (*Tetchy and frustrated but not nastily.*) It was there! Right there! Open at page eighty-three. And my notes!

JENNY (*cool*): I've got the notes. I've been working on them for you. Lenchen was reading Owen.

MARX: Women!

JENNY (*hands on hips*): Yes?

MARX: Oh, nothing!

Fade.

Scene Four – Flirtations

JENNY stepping out of a tin bath. Ties two towels around herself. Walks to a small mirror. Tries to look at her figure in it. Holds up her breasts with her hands. Adjusts strands of hair on forehead. Turns sideways. Her belly seems to protrude a little. Gives a sad smile.

JENNY: Another recruit to the cause. Numero cinque.

She takes mirror off wall. Walks to chair and sits down, back to the door which is ajar. Looks closely at her face. Bites lip. Shakes head.

JENNY: Funf! More wrinkles, Rapunzel!

WILLICH enters with a red sash tied around his waist into which is thrust a sword scabbard. He wears an old Prussian army jacket over civilian clothes. He stands at the door, watching JENNY.

WILLICH: Still as lovely as ever.

JENNY, startled, rises and moves to other side of the table, arms defensively across her bosom.

JENNY: Kapitan Willich!

WILLICH: August, please. 'Kamerad' August.

JENNY *(flustered)*: Mohr is at the library, I'm having a bath.

WILLICH: Please continue!

JENNY: Can you wait in the hall please?

WILLICH advances towards her.

JENNY: Please!

WILLICH: You are, you know, the most desirable woman of all the German émigrés.

55

JENNY (*flattered but nervous, a hint of uncertainty in her voice*): Please!

WILLICH (*leaning across the table*): Such green eyes, such aristocratic grace.

JENNY: Willich! We're middle aged. We grow old in exile.

WILLICH: The prime of life. And it's so short.

He reaches across the table and touches her chin, lifting her head.

JENNY: Stand over there, with your face to the wall.

WILLICH: Oh, not the hall, then?

JENNY: You were a Prussian officer. And a gentleman. Where's all that gone?

WILLICH (*he slowly comes to attention*): One should seize the moment.

JENNY: If anyone were to return, you'd look so foolish.

WILLICH considers the remark. Turns. Walks to door and faces it. Hands on hips.

WILLICH: There. How's that?

JENNY starts to dress, not taking her eyes off him.

WILLICH: You know, for a communist, you're really rather prudish.

JENNY: It's called dignity, Herr Kapitan.

WILLICH: Dignity? Or indecision? (*Turns head slightly.*)

JENNY: I was once engaged to a Prussian officer. I know the type.

WILLICH: Oh him! Lieutenant von Pannewitz. Or should I say

Major?

JENNY: Major?

WILLICH: In Barmen, on the barricades. He was on the other side. (*Pulls sabre. JENNY is now dressed.*) I put this through the bastard's right arm. (*He turns. Flicks the arm of her dress.*) Herr Engels, my adjutant, was by my side.

JENNY: You can put your weapon away now.

WILLICH sheathes the sabre.

JENNY: So, my old fiancé's still alive?

WILLICH: He has the luck of a royalist cretin. I did it for you, for the revolution!

JENNY (*chuckles fondly*): You old romantic!

WILLICH seizes her by the shoulders and kisses her. She struggles to push him off and she pulls the sword from his scabbard.

WILLICH: Ah! A duel! (*Chuckles to himself and struts around ignoring her stance.*) My God! To think you've been reduced to this, a Soho pigsty! You could have done so much better for yourself!

JENNY: I would choose no other life. Nothing!

WILLICH: He doesn't deserve you. You're a real revolutionary at heart, not a library assistant!

JENNY: Herr Kapitan. You're getting insolent.

WILLICH: You also are lovely.

JENNY lunges at him with sword, 'stabbing' him in the right arm, pleased with herself.

WILLICH (*laughs loudly, unmoved*): Touché! Revenge for your first true love? I'll tell the Major next time we meet, that you're still hot for him, if he lives.

JENNY: Fools live forever.

WILLICH (*walks to table, flips over papers*): My God! Look at this lot! Futile philosophising, verbal constipation. It's enough to give you a headache or a pain in the bum. Both, perhaps!

JENNY: If Mohr saw you touching his things he'd put you down like a dog!

WILLICH: That's not very comradely. Whatever happened to 'natural communism', everything shared? (*Looks her up and down, lewdly.*)

JENNY: I'll tell Mohr you called.

WILLICH: Don't tell him everything. (*Again, eyeing her.*) Keep your options open, my princess.

JENNY: Go!

WILLICH: Soon we'll all be going. Germany is about to explode into revolution. It's imminent.

He walks to the door. His tone now changes. He is peeved and wants to reassert his authority.

WILLICH: Tell our great leader, when he can get his schnozzle out of a book, that we don't like the venue (*looks around distastefully*) of the committee meeting. It's not a good idea to meet in people's homes.

JENNY: My sentiments entirely!

WILLICH: It gives an unfair territorial advantage to certain 'factions'. (*He comes smartly to attention. Clicks heels. Bows slowly and stares at her, holding the sword.*)

WILLICH: Ah, Kameradschaft! (*Turns, marches out, laughing loudly.*)

Fade.

Scene Five – Second Fiddle

Downstage, with the rear set in darkness. Engels' fine house in Manchester. There is an elegant writing desk and fireplace. ENGELS is an endearing character. He is fair haired, medium stature, athletic. He speaks quickly with a suggestion of a stammer. As the scene opens, the two are walking diagonally top left to downstage right, in opposite directions, hands behind backs. The 'Sherlock Holmes & Doctor Watson' should be underplayed. The 'political' dialogue should be rapid, to emphasise the relationship between the two men, rather than the content.

ENGELS: So why is Malthus wrong?

MARX: My dear Friedrich. The so called 'laws' governing land rent are merely laws of bourgeois competition.

ENGELS: Based on the interplay of prices in the capitalist market.

MARX: Exit Malthus. Stake through the heart! The stinking corpse can now be buried.

ENGELS: It won't stop the necrophiliacs lurking round his tomb.

MARX: If that's how they get their intellectual pleasure, I wish them every disease they deserve. (*Waves hand.*) Noch 'ne Flasche!

ENGELS breaks off to open a bottle of wine. He pours as MARX continues to criss-cross the room. ENGELS hands him a glass and resumes his diagonal.

MARX: My further investigations lead me to conclude that the influx of precious metals do not determine the trade balance nor exchange rates on the world money market.

ENGELS: Classical theory is erroneous?

MARX: It's a bucket of shit! (*He swigs back the whole glass. Slams it down. Resumes vigorous walking.*)

ENGELS: So if the culprit isn't gold, what is?

MARX: From my studies, the evidence suggests that Robert Owen, Fielden, Hopkins, all the English socialists, have overlooked one vital clue. Look! What is the determinant of investment?

ENGELS: Why, the rate of return on capital?

MARX: And what determines the rate of return?

ENGELS: The value obtained from labour. Look, what...

MARX: And this spurs on our bourgeois to invest, invest, invest! There comes a point, my dear Engels, when this immense accumulation of capital comes into conflict with the restraints of the social relations of production.

ENGELS (*irritated*): But, we're both perfectly aware of all this!

MARX (*firmly*): But we didn't know, and we didn't know when.

ENGELS: 'When?'

MARX: It's imminent. Here in England, there will be an economic crisis of revolutionary proportions within weeks!

ENGELS: Weeks! Then should we not return to London immediately?

MARX (*holding up glass*): Not that imminent!

ENGELS pours.

MARX: Those idiot Germans! That loud-mouthed, muddle-headed, impotent, émigré, London rabble. They think that Germany will be the first to blow! It's not Germany! It's England. And America, the most advanced economies.

MARX drinks up. ENGELS refills glasses.

ENGELS: It's so good to have these discussions. I really miss them. I'm isolated, here in Manchester.

MARX: Well, you've got a fine house, a good life!

ENGELS: How can you say that after what we've been discussing. It could 'blick' like a pricked bubble.

MARX: Dear Friedrich! You're not hankering for a bourgeois existence are you?

ENGELS: I tolerate it Mohr. I tolerate it. I just don't want it to go on too long. Do you know I'm even expected to go hunting.

MARX (*laughs*): You!

ENGELS: Yes! (*Drinks up.*) It's the 'done thing'. Tally ho! 'I say fellows, there goes the bushy-tailed blighter! After him! What ho!'

MARX: Sounds great fun! I'd love to. (*Rises.*) How do you think I'd look on a horse?

ENGELS: Wouldn't do your carbuncles any good!

MARX (*flinches, holds bum*): Don't say that! The very mention!

ENGELS: And these bourgeois women – the married ones. I can see 'natural communism' flashing in their downward glances. And I'm just the man to give it to them.

MARX: That joker Willich, your sabre-rattling friend, he's been after my Jenny!

ENGELS: Looking for the worm that wriggles in every marriage.

MARX: I'll cut his worm off for him, the swashbuckling shagomaniac. I'll take his balls to the pawnshop!

ENGELS: They're old and wrinkled.

MARX: Revolution for Willich is like one huge ejaculation. He wants to 'come' all over the barricades.

ENGELS jumps up on chair. Pulls imaginary sabre, smacks back of head repeatedly.

ENGELS: 'Fur Deutschland und der Revolution!' (*Makes humping action with his hips. The two laugh.*)

MARX: And he's an anti-semite. He's worse than me! (*Laughs.*) Fred! You're a tonic. Let's get pissed. Come on! Let's blow out all the street lamps like we used to. Give the cops a run for their money!

ENGELS (*pretending to be a cop, blows an imaginary whistle*): 'Halt in the name of the law! I say, sir!' Do you remember?

MARX: I was rat-arsed that night! Hab' den Arschvoll gehabt!

ENGELS: Two fat bobbies wobbling down Haverstock Hill. Peep! Peep!

MARX: Come on then!

ENGELS: Can't!

MARX: Come on! I'll pay!

ENGELS: You'll pay. With whose Geld?

MARX: 'From each according to his abilities...'

ENGELS (*cuts in*): Thank you!

MARX: Your Geld, you vicious exploiter of the working class, you Millgrinder! Knauseriger Jude!

ENGELS (*takes offence, turns away*): All right! That's enough!

MARX (*appeasing*): Fred!

ENGELS: You go too far!

MARX: Let's find a pub!

ENGELS (*turns his back. Quietly and introspectively*): I don't like this 'role'. Provider. Santa Klaus. Bank balancer. It doesn't come easy to me. I know even how that clown Willich feels. They were great days in Barmen. (*Emotionally.*) And we were that close! And he was a brave man. Don't forget it. And now? Reduced to gigolo! You know what he really wants to do? To fight in America to free the nigger slaves!

MARX: America wouldn't exist without niggers!

ENGELS: I don't think it is imminent. You see, we might have to wait a lifetime. You in your libraries, me in my counting house, counting out the money. Have you ever thought we might all die in England? Be buried in some quiet English graveyard where the blackbirds sing, in exile from the nucleus of the world. Dear old Deutschland.

MARX: Come! You're getting maudlin'. More wine. (*Places hands on his shoulders.*)

ENGELS: My position means I can't blow out the street lamps tonight, Mohr. There's too much at stake. Your work comes first. My money. (*He turns. MARX embraces him. Brightening up.*) I'm your old second fiddle! Of course, we could get thoroughly ratted here! (*Smiles.*)

MARX: An excellent idea, my dear Friedrich.

ENGELS: Jenkins! Another crate of Rheinisch!

Fade.

Scene Six – Kameradschaft

LENCHEN is clearing MARX's table and arranging chairs for the committee meeting. Enter WILLICH. He creeps up behind her and puts his hands over her eyes.

LENCHEN: Stop foolin' around Charley. Not now!

WILLICH (*shakes head*): Uhuh!

LENCHEN: Konrad?

WILLICH (*shakes head*): Uhuh!

He moves his hands down to her breasts. She pulls away.

LENCHEN: August, you randy old bugger!

WILLICH tries to kiss her.

LENCHEN (*lightly dismissive*): Gerroff, find someone your own age. (*She runs round other side of the table.*) Your sabre's hanging out!

WILLICH (*looks down at his flies*): Ach!

WILLICH circles table. LENCHEN provocatively runs her hands down over her breasts to her crotch and thighs.

WILLICH: I can feel the revolutionary spirit rising within me, 'citoyen et vagabonde'!

LENCHEN (*raises fingers to her nose*): Da da der-da da!

WILLICH chases her round the table. Enter SCHRAMM, a younger man. WILLICH regains composure, smooths hair back, but still jocular.

WILLICH (*ironically clicks his heels*): Herr Schramm!

SCHRAMM: 'Kamerad' please! Why so formal?

WILLICH (*holding out arms appealingly*): Konrad!

LENCHEN runs to SCHRAMM, kissing him on both cheeks.

LENCHEN: My Hotspur!

SCHRAMM: My Lady in Waiting! When are we to be married?

SCHRAMM twirls LENCHEN around.

LENCHEN (*playfully*): First we must escape from the castle of the dark Mohr, who keeps me locked up here, slaving for him!

WILLICH: I thought you had more taste Lenchen – an older man, like me. (*Twirls his moustache.*) Sophisticated, blooded in the struggle, yet still full of youthful fire!

SCHRAMM: Listen to Falstaff!

WILLICH (*playfully puts hand on sword-hilt*): Konrad is in the pay of the evil Moor! He'll not assist your escape!

Enter MARX. Looks at them all suspiciously. Changes mood of the gathering.

MARX: Children's games, eh?

WILLICH: A little romance. You take life too seriously my friend.

MARX (*approaches him*): 'Friend?'

WILLICH: As you wish!

Enter JENNY.

WILLICH (*clicks heels*): Frau Marx.

JENNY: Why all the noise? I've been trying to get the children to sleep.

LENCHEN: Come on. Let's sort the chairs out!

They all do. Except WILLICH, because there aren't enough chairs.

WILLICH: I'll stand.

MARX: Always want to be different, don't you, August?

WILLICH shrugs, indicating the lack of a chair. They sit. Apart from WILLICH who stands apart. LENCHEN takes a seat at the back.

MARX: Are we ready. Item one: England.

WILLICH (*interrupting*): What's this, a set up? Your wife's not on the Committee, nor your housekeeper.

MARX: Observers!

SCHRAMM: We're all comrades surely?

WILLICH: No voting rights then!

MARX: Can we proceed?

WILLICH (*perambulating. Swift delivery*): Yes. A new revolution is imminent in Germany. The League must prepare for the seizure of power. We need a tight, secret organisation. London is crawling with Prussian spies. Secrecy is essential.

MARX (*stands*): Did you not hear us? Item one: England, the movement for reform!

WILLICH (*ignoring him*): Huh! 'Reform!' Kameraden! The German working class...

MARX: That is not the order of business. (*Firmly.*) The German revolution is not on the agenda.

WILLICH (*open mouthed with disbelief. Looks around*): Not! Let's wait for Kamerad Engels. Tell him that to his face.

JENNY: He won't be here.

WILLICH: Not here? Why not?

JENNY: Business matters in Manchester.

WILLICH: My God! So now 'business' comes before revolution! I suppose he's busy humping his Irish mill-hands!

JENNY: Is sex all you think about!

WILLICH: Kamerad Engels agrees with me on the German question. I'll bet you haven't even told him about this meeting!

SCHRAMM (*earnestly pleading*): Kamerad, the German revolution is in retreat. Only through the development of theory was it possible for us to predict the revolutions in Frankfurt, Venice, Budapest.

WILLICH: It's past your bedtime Konrad! Predict! Predict! We made it happen. With swords not crystal balls!

LENCHEN: Don't waste your breath, Konrad. This man lives from day to day.

JENNY: None of us have ever been to Venice, or Budapest. How do you explain that?

LENCHEN: He thinks we started it on our holidays. What was it you once said? 'Revolutions are like women: find 'em, fuck 'em and forget 'em!'

JENNY: Really! Let's try to keep this civilised.

MARX: Look. Look! Revolution is not just a matter of swords. Even a sword has to be conceived, designed. The man who wields it must first know what it is he's fighting for. In '48 there was no shortage of revolutionary opportunities. They burst out everywhere. That time will come again. But let's be frank. They failed. Without exception. Plenty of swords. No clarity of purpose! We're not just swordsmiths. We're midwives to an era struggling to be born.

WILLICH: Midwives! Count me out! Me? Sit around while you produce a gospel for the promised land! (*Mocking.*) The God of History whispers in the lughole and you, like Moses from the mountain, bring down the ten commandments! 'Thou shalt not fart'. Still, you've got the right credentials. Half your family are Rabbis. Got a handsome brow. Look good in alabaster. I can see it now! A million serfs upon their knees give thanks to Moses Marx for Liberation! (*Coarse laughter.*) A million icons and the pong of incense. Jesus Christ – he was another one!

MARX: So cynical. So soon. All this invective can't conjure up a German revolution where there is none.

WILLICH: Oh! And who says so?

MARX: The objective laws of economic development say so. It's not a matter of what this person or that person thinks.

WILLICH: And now, I suppose, we are to be treated to your latest hobby horse Kamerad Marx. The imminence of economic crisis in England and America. There is imminence and imminence, it seems. The imminence of the German revolution is inadmissible. Why? Because it is not Doktor Marx's imminence. He prefers another imminence, an English imminence! And why? Because now Doktor Marx lives in England and world historical development, as we all know, revolves around the precise geographical location of Doktor Marx at any moment in time.

MARX: All right. You decide the agenda. I will not be provoked.

WILLICH: Item one: the accounts of the German Refugee Fund.

(*Takes paper from pocket.*) To be exact, the whereabouts of some twenty pounds!

JENNY looks alarmed. Glances at MARX.

Silence.

WILLICH: Any comments, Herr Doktor?

MARX: It was a loan.

WILLICH: To whom?

MARX: A German refugee. To myself. It will be paid back.

WILLICH: I see. Next item. Item two: the need for secrecy in our affairs.

MARX: Which 'affairs' had you in mind Kamerad Willich – political or 'personal'?

WILLICH: To be precise, the arrest of our German comrades in Köln.

MARX: Their plans for a secret uprising are premature. It's foolhardy.

WILLICH: May I finish?

MARX: Go on!

WILLICH (*looking at JENNY*): Ferdinand von Westphalen, Minister for the Interior in the Prussian Government.

JENNY: I am not responsible for my brother, his politics or his actions!

WILLICH: My point is how come Herr von Westphalen knew the whereabouts of our German comrades? Mysterious, don't you think?

SCHRAMM (*rising and pounding the table*): That's outrageous! Are you suggesting...?

MARX: Sit down Schramm!

WILLICH: I'm not suggesting anything. Only that we have it from 'Kamerad' Marx himself in what low regard he holds 'secret' organisations, 'abortive' uprisings, secrecy in general!

SCHRAMM (*rushing at WILLICH*): So ein Arschloch!

WILLICH (*threatening, hand on sword*): Ein Arschloch?

MARX (*stands up, pushes SCHRAMM*): Hier ist es wie im Zoo! Don't be provoked by these posturings!

WILLICH: We're talking about life and death!

MARX: You are talking about life and death. We are talking about patient, revolutionary work!

WILLICH: From the safety of the reading room at the British Museum, using funds filched from the refugees account with the odd letter to your brother-in-law about your 'muddle-headed' comrades in Köln!

MARX: And where do you spend your time when I'm working? Barging into people's homes...

JENNY: Mohr! No!

MARX: To molest their wives, you strutting cockerel!

WILLICH takes glove from pocket, throws it at MARX's feet.

JENNY (*quietly*): Kameraden! Please!

MARX spits on the gauntlet, refuses to pick it up. WILLICH dashes forward, drawing his sabre. SCHRAMM goes to pick up the gauntlet.

LENCHEN: No! Konrad, No! Don't!

SCHRAMM picks it up. Face to face with WILLICH.

SCHRAMM: So ein Arschloch!

SCHRAMM hands the gauntlet to WILLICH, accepting the challenge.

WILLICH: Choose your weapons!

SCHRAMM: Pistols!

JENNY: Duelling is illegal in England!

SCHRAMM: In Flanders then, Ostend. Appoint your second!

WILLICH clicks heels and exits.

Blackout.

Scene Seven – Loyalty

The duelling episode takes place rear stage, preferably on a raised platform, whilst JENNY and LENCHEN sit in darkness, front stage.

Enter front right, WILLICH and his SECOND. Enter front left, SCHRAMM and his SECOND. The two SECONDS meet centre stage with a case of pistols, which they examine. SCHRAMM'S SECOND takes first choice. They return to their corners. SCHRAMM and WILLICH walk towards each other, pistols pointing downwards and stand back to back.

REFEREE: Are you ready, gentlemen? Five paces, turn and fire.

WILLICH and SCHRAMM point pistols upwards. They walk five paces to the opposite ends of stage. They turn, face each other, pistols still pointing upwards, and shout proudly:

WILLICH: For the Communist Manifesto!

SCHRAMM: Workers of the World, Unite!

They fire. SCHRAMM falls, wounded in the head, and is attended by his SECOND, who drags him off. WILLICH and his SECOND leave, having put on their overcoats.

Lights down on back stage, lights up front stage on JENNY and LENCHEN in the Marx flat again. JENNY and LENCHEN, preoccupied with thoughts of the duel, not working but anxiously walking around room.

JENNY: We shouldn't have allowed it!

LENCHEN: There was no stopping 'em.

JENNY: Konrad's so young, so inexperienced. He's never handled a pistol in his life.

LENCHEN: Willich should be ashamed of himself – bully!

JENNY: I feel responsible.

LENCHEN: They're both grown men, it's not your fault.

JENNY: It is, partly. One morning, you were out. Willich made advances towards me.

LENCHEN: Did he now?

JENNY: I told Mohr. He flew into a rage, even questioned my faithfulness.

LENCHEN: So that's why.

JENNY: It's part of it.

LENCHEN: And I thought Konrad might be showing off for my benefit. Men!

JENNY: Dear Konrad. He's so loyal to Mohr. He would die for him!

Tears. LENCHEN comforts her. Enter MARX, moody but truculent.

MARX: Why are you crying? Any news?

LENCHEN: No, nothing.

MARX: Idioten! We've got twelve members only and two of them are shooting each other! We'll be down to ten, if they aim straight, eleven at best.

JENNY: What does that matter!

MARX: We'll be a laughing stock! The leadership of the proletariat groping around in the mists of Ostend, intent on blowing each other's brains out – if they've got any!

LENCHEN: Konrad did it for your honour!

MARX: Are you in your right mind? Your head's full of Walter Scott! Ivanhoe meets Don Quixote! Blam! Guts all over the floor! (*Acting a fairy princess.*) 'He did it for me! My Prince.' (*Throws handkerchief.*)

JENNY: You're a cold-blooded man!

MARX: Grow up the pair of you! Look at you. I do believe you're enjoying it. It reaffirms your feminine charms. You waiting for Willich to return...

JENNY: That's ignoble!

MARX: And you for your precious Konrad.

LENCHEN: Konrad's an honourable man!

MARX: Honour! Nobility! Are we living in the same world? We're up to our eyes in shit. Look at this place! It's like a painting by Hieronymos Bosch! The Garden of Delights, and below us Dwarfalberich waits for three weeks rent – again! The fare to Ostend would have paid that three times over!

JENNY: Stop it! Stop it! Stop it! Who do you think it is manages this place, fights off the creditors? We do, Lenchen and I.

LENCHEN (*bursts into tears*): Don't fight please.

JENNY: We organise your existence for you. And you make fun of us, cynical criticism, snide remarks.

MARX: Don't nag me woman! Tears and hysteria. I'll get another headache. Gott! I can feel it coming on.

MARX throws chair at wall. Smashes a cup.

MARX: This shithouse! This hellhole inferno!

JENNY: You're ungrateful, selfish. You don't appreciate me! I've tried and I've failed!

MARX walks to table. Sits down holding head. Chair gives way. Adjusts it.

MARX: I'm... sorry.

LENCHEN: I should think so!

MARX (*quietly*): I'm sorry to both of you.

MARX is holding his head. JENNY and LENCHEN are quietly sobbing. ENGELS puts his head around door.

ENGELS: Surprise! Surprise! Guess who? It's Santa Klaus!

ENGELS gallops in, wearing black riding hat and red hunting jacket, with sack of goodies. Blows hunting horn. They all look at him amazed and then burst into laughter.

MARX (*wipes tears from face, greets him*): General! What do you look like! Good to see you, Fred!

LENCHEN (*kisses ENGELS*): We've nothing to offer you. We're skint!

ENGELS (*claps hands*): Damask table cloth! Quick!

JENNY (*coolly and politely, but with a smile*): Herr Engels!

ENGELS (*organising the women*): Best silver plate and napkins! A special occasion! Your finest silver cutlery!

Quickly, the table is set.

ENGELS (*dipping into hamper*): Smoked salmon, caviare, best French bread, the finest Rheinisch wine, cold pheasant, some German sausage. (*Hands it suggestively to LENCHEN. Turns to JENNY.*) And I bought you some crystal! (*To MARX.*) And you, you lazy devil, open the wine!

MARX does so. ENGELS pours four glasses and raises his own.

ENGELS: Kameraden, may I, on this auspicious occasion, propose a toast. To...

The other three all walk away from the table, left, right, and centre.

ENGELS: What's up now?

MARX (*back to him*): You haven't heard?

ENGELS: Heard what?

JENNY (*back to him*): Willich!

LENCHEN: And Konrad Schramm.

ENGELS: What about them?

MARX: A duel.

ENGELS (*puts glass down*): Ah well! 'Bang' goes the party! Oh sorry! Time for a little serenade. (*Blows horn.*)

JENNY: Herr Engels!

ENGELS: Meine Damen und Herren.

MARX: Pack it in Fred! You're pissed!

ENGELS: May I present, tonight, our special guest, who will display to you, for your entertainment, his skill with the pistols. Herr Konrad Schramm, give him a big hand!

Enter SCHRAMM with bandaged head. The women rush to SCHRAMM and embrace him. MARX shakes his hand. ENGELS sits down and tucks in, ignoring them.

JENNY: Herr Schramm!

LENCHEN: Konrad!

SCHRAMM kisses LENCHEN.

LENCHEN: You're wounded!

SCHRAMM: Just a graze, nothing really.

MARX: You're a brave man Konrad. Come, drink!

They all sit down on makeshift chairs, chatting excitedly and knocking back the wine. Another bottle is taken from the hamper.

LENCHEN: Speech! Speech!

SCHRAMM (*rises*): I'll keep it short. I aimed for the end of his pimmel and hit him on his left boot!

ALL (*applause*): Bravo!

SCHRAMM: I give you a toast. To Karl Marx, our liberator and our leader!

ALL: Speech!

MARX (*rises, playing up to it humorously*): A few words on the subject of Ricardo's theory of rent!

ALL: Oh no!

ENGELS: Don't tell me! How many weeks do you owe?

JENNY: Three!

ENGELS: Well, you don't any more! I met old Rabin on the stairs and paid him off for the next two months! So! Let's eat, drink and be merry!

Cheers all round.

Fade.

Scene Eight – Chessmate

MARX is working at his desk, with a bottle of wine and smoking a pipe. On the floor, a half-played chess game. Enter LENCHEN, busy, cleaning.

MARX: Quiet! Quiet!

LENCHEN: Sorry.

She continues working.

MARX (*to himself*): Money buys the commodity, Labour. 'M' equals 'C'. 'C' becomes money again, but this time M+. Why? Because... there is a missing factor! A missing factor. Labour, the commodity, produces more than its own value...

LENCHEN: It's past midnight.

MARX (*writing*): More than its own value. Surplus value! (*Stands.*) Lenchen! Lenchen, read this.

LENCHEN: Is this in German or English? Your writing is definitely the worst I've ever seen. (*Puts head in an arc to follow slope of the writing.*)

MARX (*excited*): Read it! Read it!

LENCHEN: I'm tired, Charley.

Snatches paper from her, excitedly. Throws it on table. Grabs LENCHEN by the shoulders and 'places' her.

MARX: Look! Pretend you are a worker...

LENCHEN: Cheeky sod! I am a bloody worker.

MARX fills his glass and swigs. He hams Jewish mannerisms as he acts out this little part.

MARX: Whilst I am a bourgeois, in the, er, chair manufacturing business. (*Strokes beard. Flashes eyes.*) How about coming back to my place and I'll increase your wages?

LENCHEN (*playing the simple country girl*): Well, I don't know master, I'm sure.

MARX: Ah! (*Spots a chair.*) I see you have made a chair!

LENCHEN: Well it is a chair factory, master. Seemed like the right thing to do.

MARX: Excellent! And you made this chair, in one whole day, shall we say, all by yourself!

LENCHEN (*curtsies*): With my own fair hands, Sir!

MARX: And your wages for that one whole day are?

LENCHEN drops act momentarily.

LENCHEN: You don't pay me wages, Charley!

MARX: Six pence a day I think we agreed.

LENCHEN (*resumes the act*): Aye master. Six pence, master.

MARX: Now, my pretty one! (*Holds her chin and slips coin into her hand.*) This chair. Market price, one shilling. I'd like you to do a very simple thing for me.

LENCHEN: Well I am very simple, Sir.

MARX: I want you, with your day's wages, to buy this product of your day's work, from me.

LENCHEN gives him sixpence. Grabs chair.

LENCHEN: Fair exchange is no robbery.

MARX (*holding heart with mock shock*): Oy-yoy-oy! What's this, already! Six pence! Thief! Call the police. This chair is worth one shilling.

LENCHEN: Right, then! I made it! You owes me sixpence more!

MARX (*drops act*): Got it! Surplus value! (*Starts perambulating excitedly.*) The original sin of the whole thieving edifice! The worm in the apple. In that one simple act of exchange is contained the stinking morality of the whole system. (*Takes her by the shoulders.*) A crime against humanity!

79

LENCHEN: Charley! You're sweating and shaking. (*She takes his hand.*)

MARX: All this week, while Jenny's been away...

LENCHEN: No Charley, I've got things to do, and, (*she pulls herself away*) and anyway...

MARX: Lenchen, please.

LENCHEN: Why don't you have a drink perhaps. I could do with one.

She pours him one and one for herself.

MARX: A poor substitute. (*He grabs her wrist.*)

LENCHEN: Here! (*Diverting him.*) You know you're in check, don't you?

MARX: Me! In check?

LENCHEN: You have been since three o'clock this afternoon.

MARX rushes to board, spread-eagles himself on the floor.

MARX: I'll soon sort you out, Miss Demuth! There! My king's bishop's pawn to three.

LENCHEN: That'll put you in check from my Bishop.

MARX: You mean you can play without looking at the board!

LENCHEN: Try me!

MARX: My queen to queen's bishop four. (*Makes the move.*)

LENCHEN (*without looking*): Your queen's had it, mate! It's mate in two.

MARX: You little vixen.

LENCHEN kneels at board to make final moves.

LENCHEN: My humble pawn has done for the black king.

MARX looks up slowly. They embrace. LENCHEN falls back across the board, kissing him.

MARX: Come on Lenchen! No one will ever know.

Blackout.

ACT TWO
Scene One – Nightmare

MARX on a makeshift bed, corner left. He is in a high fever, sweating, gasping, as he hallucinates.

MARX: Ach! Ach, nein! Achtung!

He relapses again into a feverish sleep for a moment, then leaps up from a vivid nightmare. He is dressed in a nightshirt. His cries awaken RABIN, the only other person in the building.

MARX *(staggers to pull curtains but it is night)*: Licht! Licht! *(Slumps to floor.)*

MARX *(grabs a razor and holds it in front of his face, then above his bared thigh, about to make a cut)*: Knauseriger Geists! Geld!

RABIN *(appears at door with candle, watches, amazed)*: Oh my Gawd!

MARX *(pointing the razor at RABIN)*: Keep away from me, Shekels!

RABIN *(advancing despite his fear)*: About the rent: forget it!

MARX: Stand back. Keep your yellow hands off me. Don't you see, we're all corrupted with it!

RABIN: Corrupted? I...

MARX: Yes, money. Foul stinking filth-Geld. Clogging up the veins with slime-gold. 'Radix malorum est cupiditas!' Look! I'm just a mass of yellow pus, erupting in a mountain range of boils and carbuncles, all over my groin, my genitals, my arse and thighs. *(In a deranged whine.)* I have to cut them open, let out the golden liquid.

RABIN: Don't do it Mr Mohr. You'll bleed to death!

MARX: Blood! I've no blood left. Some jaundice, deep inside from long ago, makes me detest myself.

RABIN: You're not that bad. All right, in fact!

MARX: You and I, we're barely human. We should be abolished, the earth cleansed of us and all our kind!

RABIN (*firmly*): You're a sick man. Sick, do you hear me?

MARX (*raises the razor to strike*): The world demands a sacrifice!

RABIN: Not in this house!

He rushes forward as MARX collapses, dropping the razor. RABIN rushes to the water jug and brings a glass to MARX. He holds MARX's head and makes him drink.

RABIN: There, it's just a fever. You're delirious, I'll fetch your housekeeper!

MARX: She's not here.

RABIN: Your wife then!

MARX: She's left me, I'm alone.

RABIN: She'll be back, upset perhaps. (*He mops MARX's brow with a handkerchief.*) You do too much thinking. Not good for a man!

RABIN pillows MARX's head in his lap and starts to pray in Hebrew, rocking back and forwards as he mumbles the prayers. He gives MARX more water.

MARX (*slowly coming round*): Danke Danke!

RABIN: It is just a dream, Mr Mohr, a horrible nightmare.

MARX (*breathing with difficulty*): Vile shadows, fantasies and monstrous shapes and things I dare not, cannot, think. Can I tell you something? You wouldn't tell a soul?

RABIN: What's to tell?

MARX: I dreamed I had a son. And he was everything a man could want and wish for, clean-limbed, bright-eyed, strong, intelligent and loving. He was hope fulfilled, redemption for millennia of the sufferings of men. A vision realised.

RABIN: Quite a son, eh?

MARX: Oh he was of my body and my flesh, though he was born, it seemed, when I was in my grave. But he was restless, full of energy, and went away from me. Oh, far, far away, he said, to found a city, on a hilltop, and he said he would use my words with which to build it. Gleaming, with spires and towers, bathed in the purest of white light. He would write and tell me of its wonders. All things held in common! A city without gold. No money, nor currency, nor any kind of wealth that might divide the rich from poor. A true equality of human virtue. Here was no greed, but love; no toil but learning; no conflict but harmony. I begged to be allowed to visit him before I died, but he bade me stay, until the time was ripe.

MARX (continuing): At last I could endure my curiosity no longer and travelled out of my tomb. Through time, it seemed, forward to the city of my son. I wanted to see with my own eyes! (He bites his lip and grimaces.) Oh Christ! As I came out from an endless desert I could see the citadels, but a smell of blood was in the air. A mighty wall confronted me composed entirely of human skulls, staring down upon a moat of gore and rotting entrails. I crossed a footbridge of maimed and mangled corpses into the heart of the city. Having no wealth my son had built his capital with bones of all the city's citizens. There was not one sign of life until he appeared, framed upon a savage altar set in the wall. His likeness to me was unmistakable. He smiled. I reached out, and touched a mirror!

MARX cries. RABIN comforts him.

MARX: I was looking at myself. For there, beneath the altar was a tomb, and on it was the name of 'Guido'!

RABIN: Don't fret!

MARX: Poor wretches then ran from their shacks of bone and sinew, fell down in front of me and cried 'Divine One! See his mighty head. A Godhead with a lion's mane!' I shouted back and my words melted into the desert air. 'Nicht Gott, Ich bin ein mann, Ich bin ein mann!'

RABIN (*after a pause during which MARX sobs*): That was some dream!

MARX: Can there be meaning in a dream?

RABIN: Always, but who are we to put constructions on it? Dreams should be kept in their place. Under the pillow. Don't let them take control!

MARX (*intrigued*): A dream that takes control.

RABIN: Becomes a nightmare, a real one!

MARX: I'm tired. I've not been well. Two nights ago, my wife and I, we quarrelled. You must have heard?

RABIN: What's to hear?

MARX: Good. Oh, this life in exile!

RABIN: Perhaps it's faith you're exiled from?

MARX: Never was a one for faith.

RABIN (*preparing to leave*): It's your sort needs it most. Life's hard. Don't expect too much from it. Struggle and endure. Expect no peace this side of death. Be thankful for your wife and lovely children. Good night Mr Mohr.

MARX: A dream that takes control!

Fade.

Scene Two – Jealousy

An autumn day. LENCHEN is reading and making notes. Enter JENNY, now very pregnant, and it shows.

JENNY (*short tempered*): What are you doing?

LENCHEN (*engrossed*): Robert Owen. Not bad stuff.

JENNY: Not now Lenchen.

LENCHEN: Hang on! Just finish this chapter.

JENNY: We can't all be reading books.

LENCHEN (*still scribbling*): One minute.

JENNY (*busying herself*): The children's clothes are piling up.

LENCHEN (*underlines some words in book*): Aha!

JENNY: I was up till two last night, copying out articles. And my little Guido's sick. He needs the doctor. We've no money to pay him. (*Getting tearful.*) Give me that! (*Snatches book from LENCHEN.*)

LENCHEN: Jenny! Please!

JENNY (*very upset*): I can't cope. Look at me!

LENCHEN (*comforting her*): I'm sorry. I...

JENNY: Oh Lenchen, what kind of life is this?

LENCHEN: Sit down. I'll make some tea.

JENNY (*pulling away*): No, I'm going to fetch the doctor. Guido is dying. I swear it!

LENCHEN: Don't say that!

JENNY: It's true! (*She moves towards door.*) He can't go on suffering like this, taking in blood with his milk. (*Exits. Shouts.*) I shan't be long. (*Returns. Takes some silver spoons from the mantlepiece. There is still some plate left. Exits.*)

LENCHEN rises. Walks to table. Holds stomach. Rushes to corner and is violently sick, panting and heaving.

LENCHEN: Oh my God! Oh God! What am I to do? This will kill her, she'll never survive it. (*Holds her belly.*) If only you would die. Let Guido live and you die, traitor within me. No! No! I didn't mean it. Please, I didn't mean that!

Enter SCHRAMM, buoyant, with flowers. LENCHEN cries quietly to herself, rocking as if holding her baby.

SCHRAMM: Lenchen!

LENCHEN (*startled, dries her eyes guiltily*): Oh come in, come in.

SCHRAMM: Are you all right?

LENCHEN: It's nothing.

SCHRAMM: You're sick?

LENCHEN: I drank sour milk, always makes me heave.

SCHRAMM (*offers flowers*): For you!

LENCHEN (*tearful again*): Oh Konrad! (*Sinks head in his chest.*) You're such a good man!

SCHRAMM: There is something the matter. Tell me, I'll do anything for you. You know that.

LENCHEN: Would you really, Konrad?

SCHRAMM (*with youthful ardour*): Of course. In fact I have a confession to make. The duel with Willich, that wasn't just for Mohr's honour. It was for you.

LENCHEN: For me?

SCHRAMM: When I saw Willich with his arm around you, I...

LENCHEN: And you survived! A cat with nine lives. Remember when we were being evicted and you rode off on the nearest horse to get help?

SCHRAMM: The damn thing bolted, dragged me along by the stirrups!

LENCHEN: When they brought you back we laid you down on the floor with the babies.

SCHRAMM: Like a field hospital after battle.

LENCHEN: I thought you were a goner then.

SCHRAMM: You bathed my wounds, mopped my brow. That's when I knew.

LENCHEN: Knew?

SCHRAMM (*turning away shyly, hands in pockets*): I can't stand these empty-headed English women. For me, it's got to be a good German girl.

LENCHEN: Konrad, I don't know what to say.

MARX (*voice off*): Jenny! Jenny! Where are you? (*Entering.*) Oh. (*Jealously.*) I trust I'm not interrupting anything.

SCHRAMM and LENCHEN are embarrassed and draw apart to opposite sides of the room.

LENCHEN: I'm sorry.

MARX: What are we running here, a bordello? Every time I turn my back, someone comes around to do some propositioning!

LENCHEN: Charley!

MARX: Don't 'Charley' me! This place is filthy. Look at it!

LENCHEN leaves to do some work.

SCHRAMM: That was a little harsh wasn't it?

MARX: Sit down. I want to talk to you.

SCHRAMM (*puzzled*): What is the matter?

MARX: Oh sit down and pin your ears back!

SCHRAMM sits. MARX paces around.

MARX (*fast delivery*): Willich and Schapper have formed their own group. To all intents and purposes there are now two Communist Leagues. They plan a rally and a banquet for the anniversary of the February Revolution. The Chartists are invited. We're not! But we're going anyway.

SCHRAMM: Uninvited guests?

MARX: Precisely! I want you to go.

SCHRAMM: If I must.

MARX: Be careful. I wouldn't put anything past them. These are violent men. Willich is crazy, as you well know.

SCHRAMM: Is this wise?

MARX: It's necessary we are represented.

Pause.

SCHRAMM: All right. I'll do it!

Now that he's won a favour from SCHRAMM, MARX is a little more conciliatory, but still scheming.

MARX: And Konrad, try not to visit my house during the day when I'm not here.

SCHRAMM: But...

MARX: The women have work to do. Understand, they're very 'edgy' at the moment. You know women.

SCHRAMM: Only...

MARX: Have I your word on it? (*Holds out hand.*)

SCHRAMM: Yes.

They shake hands.

SCHRAMM: Shall I go armed to the rally?

MARX: No, no, no. Keep in the background. Listen to what is said, make mental notes. So, no more meetings with Lenchen, eh?

SCHRAMM (*head sinks*): I'll think about it. (*Exits.*)

Blackout.

Scene Three – Gestation

JENNY, very pregnant, reading a letter. Angry about contents. Enter MARX.

JENNY: What's the meaning of this?

MARX (*tired*): Of what?

JENNY: This! (*Hands him letter.*) From Frankfurt. Herr Weydemeyer.

MARX: What's he up to? (*Scans letter.*)

JENNY: Not what he's up to. What you're up to!

MARX: Oh that!

JENNY: You owe me an explanation.

MARX: I owe you what?

JENNY: You wrote to Weydemeyer without my permission.

MARX: Your permission!

JENNY: Instructing him to sell my family silver.

MARX: 'Your family' – since when this preoccupation with private property?

JENNY: I demand to be consulted.

MARX: Oh! Forgive me. I forgot we had a bourgeois marriage. I thought we were communists. Goods in common, a relationship of equals?

JENNY: How can it be equal when I am not consulted?

MARX: Right! I'm consulting you. Can we sell your family silver?

JENNY: That's an ultimatum, a fait accompli!

MARX: It really doesn't take very much for all the old birthmarks to show through, does it? The selfish individualism, the concern with trinkets and trivia.

JENNY: Who do you think you are you talking to? Don't you dare adopt that haughty tone with me. I who work and slave for you, share your self-imposed poverty, tolerate your total irresponsibility with money!

MARX: Work, for me? What unadulterated bourgeois claptrap! For me? Why do you think I am doing this? For myself? Be a bourgeois if you must but please don't extend your mealy-mouthed motives to me!

JENNY (*angrier*): You can't speak to me like this! I who care for you.

MARX (*bellowing*): I don't care about myself. Don't you understand that yet? I don't care!

JENNY (*standing up to him*): All right then! But you've no right not to care about others. Even your own mother you treat like dirt.

MARX (*lowering his voice*): Leave her out of this.

JENNY: You drew a bill on her account without her permission, and now she won't speak to us.

MARX: She's sitting on the filth-Geld, accumulating interest like a boil.

JENNY: She'll cut you out of the inheritance.

MARX: Oh! So that's what's bothering you, Frau Altruist, Princess Philanthropy.

JENNY: You don't care about me! You don't care about anybody!

MARX: Guido needs a doctor! And you're gabbling on about family silver!

JENNY: Get out! Get out! Your father was right about you, but I wouldn't listen!

MARX: I'm going. (*Heads for door.*)

JENNY: You're never here to see the child, and now you blame me.

MARX: I'll return when you're in a more rational state!

MARX slams door. JENNY throws book at it and collapses in tears at the desk. Enter LENCHEN, now just visibly pregnant.

LENCHEN (*comforting her*): Please don't cry.

JENNY: I can't take much more. He's so bound up with that accursed book! It's draining the lifeblood from him, from all of us! He doesn't care about me, anything.

LENCHEN: He does care. Never doubt.

JENNY: You think so?

LENCHEN: You are the most important thing in the world to him.

JENNY: I no longer believe that.

LENCHEN: You and the children. Without you, he's lost.

JENNY: You're wrong, Lenchen.

LENCHEN (*calming her*): I'm right.

JENNY: I am the wife of some future scheme of things, wedded to a system, trying to be born. The present doesn't matter to Mohr, and I am the present. He cares more about Herr Engels than he does about me. They write to each other like lovers!

LENCHEN: That's his work.

JENNY: That's what he's married to.

LENCHEN: Mohr is isolated. He must discuss.

JENNY: Why not with me, with you? We're just hausfrauen. It's as if he has two wives.

Places her hands on LENCHEN's hair and lets it run down her body thoughtlessly. LENCHEN draws back, startled.

JENNY: Lenchen, you're putting on weight.

LENCHEN turns back on her. Fights off tears.

JENNY: Lenchen! What's the matter?

LENCHEN sobs.

LENCHEN: I... I... I'll clean the children's room.

JENNY (*quietly*): You're pregnant, aren't you?

LENCHEN stands sobbing, back to her.

JENNY: Who is it, Lenchen? Is it Konrad?

LENCHEN shakes her head, sniffing into handkerchief.

JENNY: Don't protect him. He must face up to his responsibilities.

LENCHEN: Say nothing. I will see to it.

JENNY (*with disgust*): My God! Is it Herr Engels?

LENCHEN: I... I...

JENNY (*concern, doubt*): Who then?

Commotion in the hallway outside. Door bursts open. Enter SCHRAMM, leaning on doorposts, badly beaten, blood pouring from head and mouth. He collapses at their feet.

SCHRAMM: Frau Marx!

LENCHEN (*rushing to his aid*): Konrad!

JENNY: Quick. Get him on to a blanket. Get some water! No. There's a little brandy I use for Guido.

They get SCHRAMM onto blanket, tend his wounds and give him brandy.

JENNY: Who did this to you?

SCHRAMM (*with difficulty*): Willich, Schapper and the gang. At the rally. They spotted us.

JENNY (*to LENCHEN*): Fetch the doctor. And drag Mohr out of the tavern. Find him!

Exit LENCHEN.

SCHRAMM: Am I badly hurt? I feel nothing in my arm.

JENNY: And they call themselves communists!

Fade.

Scene Four – Pavane

MARX is in ordinary clothing with a blanket around his shoulders. He has a bronchial coughing fit, then relapses into deep sorrow huddled against the cold. Enter JENNY, still pregnant and in mourning black. She tries desperately to retain composure. She stands, back to MARX. Pause.

JENNY: Our little Guido is at rest now.

MARX: Don't!

JENNY: Sleeping soundly at last. The certificate said meningitis. I wish, I wish... his little form, wrapped in a shroud... I wish he could have had a coffin.

95

MARX (*staring distraught, into space*): Please don't. I can't bear it!

JENNY: How's your chest? Feeling better?

MARX: I have no right to feel better.

JENNY: Taken your medicine?

MARX: I don't want to get better!

JENNY: No child should suffer the way Guido did!

MARX: Don't talk about it!

JENNY: It isn't right. There were three other children buried near. No fathers, any of them. A prostitute from Wardour Street, drinks in the tavern, fifteen years old, a grieving mother.

MARX (*in anguish*): I should have gone.

JENNY: Where's the sense in that? The fog froze us to the marrow. I don't want to lose you too.

MARX: I collected his toys together.

JENNY cracks at last. With a wail she sinks to her knees. MARX rushes to comfort her. She buries her head into his chest.

MARX: My dearest! My princess!

JENNY: Oh, promise me! Promise me!

MARX: Anything!

JENNY: Promise me you'll take your medicine. If anything happened to you...

MARX: Your old Mohr will live, I'm afraid. Not that he deserves to.

JENNY: Oh Mohr, Mohr, I've been so happy. (*Tears.*) With you. Promise it will never change!

MARX: Always and for ever. I cannot live without you.

JENNY: Nor me without you. (*Trying to brighten up.*) We shall take the children away – for a holiday?

MARX: We shall. A complete rest for you.

JENNY: You'll come?

MARX: All of us. Now! You must look after yourself. (*Lifts her up.*) Here! (*Prepares a chair for her.*) Rest! I'll get you a little brandy. (*MARX moves to mantelpiece.*)

JENNY: No, it was for Guido. Two drops to help him sleep. Pour it away, please.

MARX pours brandy away.

JENNY: Thank you! (*Silence.*) Will Lenchen go?

MARX: Go?

JENNY: To the seaside with us?

MARX: Whatever you wish, my love.

JENNY: She should. Not a word to her from Herr Engels. He should be ashamed.

MARX: Have you spoken with her about this?

JENNY: About?

MARX: About the...

JENNY: She hasn't admitted to me Engels is the father. But I know.

I know it must be him. I've never liked him.

MARX: Oh!

MARX appears not to be able to breath and is seized with what must be remorse.

JENNY: Lenchen! Come quickly!

Enter LENCHEN in black, and now visibly pregnant. The two women support him, his hands around each of their shoulders.

JENNY: Get him to bed!

MARX (*muttering*): My son! My son! I want to die. I want to die. I want to die.

JENNY (*as they exit to bedroom*): Fetch the medicine, now!

Blackout.

Scene Five – Fertility

LENCHEN, six months pregnant, preparing towels and water for the impending birth of Franziska to JENNY. Enter MARX pacing up and down.

MARX: Where is that Doctor!

LENCHEN (*coolly*): He'll be here.

MARX: But the birth, it's imminent.

LENCHEN: There's a while yet. (*Lifts bowl with jug.*) Can you open the door for me?

MARX (*lost in thought*): Oh, of course.

LENCHEN exits to bedroom. MARX snaps fingers, sits down,

scribbles frantically. Re-enter LENCHEN, busily. MARX jumps up.

MARX: What do you think?

LENCHEN: Everything is as it should be.

MARX: Thank God. I hate births, you know, they make me nervous. (*Is tempted to work again.*) So much can go wrong.

LENCHEN: You've got a way with words, you know.

MARX (*sheepishly*): Oh yes.

Loud knock.

MARX: That's him. Can you get it?

LENCHEN doesn't move.

MARX: Sorry. I'll do it. I'll do it.

LENCHEN shakes head in disbelief. Continues working.

DOCTOR (*voice off*): Yes, yes, I remember the last one. You were in Chelsea then. Must have been, um...

MARX (*voice off. Impatiently*): Eighteen months ago.

They enter.

DOCTOR: Oh, a fallow year then? (*Approaching LENCHEN.*) Frau Marx! Why I'd say you've got some months to go.

MARX (*turns DOCTOR around to face door*): She's in there! My study! The delivery ward!

DOCTOR (*to LENCHEN*): Forgive me! You must be, er...

MARX: Fraulein Demuth, my housekeeper!

MARX gesticulates and nods angrily to LENCHEN to take him out. Resumes frantic scribbling. LENCHEN re-enters.

MARX (*throws down pen*): If only work were as productive as marriage.

LENCHEN: If only birth were as painless as work!

MARX: By the way, how are you feeling?

LENCHEN: Oh, wonderful. She is the woman I most love and admire.

MARX: I also. How do you think I feel?

LENCHEN: You'll survive!

MARX (*sighs*): It's no wonder babies scream when they see the light.

DOCTOR (*voice off*): Fraulein, er, you can, er, come in now.

LENCHEN exits to bedroom. MARX resumes scribbling. Suddenly the cry of a baby. MARX stands.

MARX: Please let it be a son!

DOCTOR (*entering, drying hands*): A little girl. Congratulations! (*Packing bag.*) An easy birth. Awful lot of girls this past week. Well done!

MARX: Thank you.

LENCHEN (*enters, straight to MARX*): Congratulations!

DOCTOR (*clears throat*): I have another delivery at number seventy-three, or was it thirty-seven? So, er...

MARX: Of course.

DOCTOR: Two pounds if you please, Herr Marx. Thank you, thank you. I can find my own way out. (*Exits.*)

MARX and LENCHEN stare at each other.

MARX: I must see her. (*Exits to bedroom, leaving LENCHEN alone.*)

Fade.

Scene Six – Surrogate Fathers

In Engels' fine house in Manchester. ENGELS sits behind an elegant writing desk, downstage.

SERVANT (*voice off*): Doctor Marx, Sir!

ENGELS rises immediately and moves towards door.

ENGELS: Thank you Jenkins. Show him in.

MARX brushes past the SERVANT and past ENGELS, grim-faced.

ENGELS: My dear fellow! Is something the matter?

MARX: Everything's the matter. The whole thing!

ENGELS: Come now. You exaggerate. You need a drink. (*Goes to cabinet. Fills glass with wine.*) More trouble with Willich? We'll soon sort him out. If he wants another duel, I'll fight him, and finish the old sod off.

MARX: Willich. Yes. But much worse.

ENGELS: Worse than Willich. Sounds nasty.

Hands MARX a drink. MARX gulps down whole glass. Hands it back. ENGELS looks at empty glass.

ENGELS: A subtle bouquet? Fine, full-bodied flavour? Another bucketful, Mein Herr? I was so sorry to hear about Guido. Poor little chap. The other kids are all right, I hope?

MARX: The girls are fine but Edgar's poorly. Why is it always my sons? And now there's this other business!

ENGELS (*sighing patiently*): Whatever it is, old fellow, try and separate it out from all the other problems. Get it in perspective.

MARX (*gruff, uptight*): A thing-in-itself? What kind of outlook do you call that!

ENGELS: I see. A social call, a soiree, with perhaps eine kleine nachtmusik, some sparkling repartee.

MARX: Fuck off Fred!

ENGELS (*trying hard to keep his sense of humour*): Now? Shall I go now, Herr Doktor? (*Walks to door.*) Just ring when you want me. I'll be grovelling in the scullery.

MARX: Stop arsing around.

ENGELS: Faithful Fred will never fail you, mein Führer! Your little blond, blue-eyed spaniel. One sweetly-whispered command and the schweinehund comes to heel. Raus! Raus!

MARX: Can we cut the play-acting now? (*Holds out glass for refill.*)

ENGELS: Get your own!

MARX does so mechanically, ignoring the rebuff.

ENGELS: You know, you're not the only one with problems.

MARX (*looking around the drinks cabinet and room*): I should have such problems!

ENGELS: Oh, don't come the downtrodden Prometheus with me! You chose your path. You're penniless, but you're free.

MARX (*derisive laughter*): You're very sloppy with your terminology tonight, dear General.

ENGELS: You are free in spirit.

MARX: Oh! Spirits now is it!

ENGELS: I don't want to be here. This bourgeois existence. I didn't choose it.

MARX: Spare me the sob stuff, moneybags. What's your problem?

ENGELS: You're not very understanding to your friend who loves you.

MARX (*sighs*): I'm sorry, Fred.

ENGELS: I lead two lives, three, Mohr. This one – entertaining father's business friends, the mill grinders. Then there's my work with you.

MARX: And what?

ENGELS: Another house, with Mary and Lizzie. I sleep there.

MARX: And that's a problem?

ENGELS: It is. Mary wants to marry me.

MARX: So?

ENGELS: How can I? It would be the scandal of Manchester.

MARX: Manchester needs a bloody good scandal. You'd be doing it a favour.

ENGELS: 'Son of mill owner marries illiterate Irish mill hand... and her sister.' Can you imagine?

MARX: Mmmmh. Not a good idea, really.

ENGELS: In any case, I'm not sure. You know how I love women. When one of these bourgeois wives looks at me, with her high collar, buttoned up against temptation, I ask myself what's she like, really like, when you touch the little pearl button of her blouse and her calm gives way to delicious passive frenzy. That moment when all the conventions break down, a pregnant silence!

MARX: For God's sake, don't use that word! What's the purpose of all this?

ENGELS: One woman wouldn't satisfy me.

MARX: And this is a new discovery? A breakthrough in the science of sexual dialectics?

ENGELS: You're not listening.

MARX: Why should I listen to what I already know?

ENGELS: I'm not sure whether I love Mary or her sister. Can you imagine living in a house with two attractive women so close to each other?

MARX (*nods ironically*): You poor bastard! I know exactly how you feel! Here, she's not pregnant, is she?

ENGELS: Who?

MARX: Well, either of them?

ENGELS: No.

MARX: That's a relief. No. I wouldn't marry if I were you. It's a mistake for men like us. Ties one down by a thousand petty threads to the daily striving for the minutiae of (*distastefully*) physical existence. And for women it's diabolical!

ENGELS: You and Jenny seem so happy.

MARX: She'd be happier without me.

ENGELS: She's a wonderful woman. Hates me, of course. After all these years I'm still 'Herr Engels'!

MARX: The trouble is, I need her desperately. She is my guardian angel, my confessor, my strength, my alter ego.

ENGELS: You're still in love with her.

MARX: I adore her. Without her, I couldn't function.

ENGELS: She feels the same?

MARX: Perhaps not for long.

ENGELS: What do you mean?

MARX: Noch 'ne Flasche.

ENGELS fetches another bottle, already opened. MARX stands up. Pours two glasses as ENGELS sits.

ENGELS (*taking drink from MARX*): You! Waiting on me! This is serious.

MARX (*long pause*): It's Lenchen.

ENGELS: Ah Lenchen! My little serving wench. She's all right, I hope? I've always loved her dearly.

MARX: How dearly?

ENGELS: I'd do anything for that girl, for all of you. You know that.

MARX: So would she. I have her word on it.

ENGELS: Spit it out, old fellow!

MARX walks to window. Back to ENGELS, glass in hand.

MARX: A little bit of... pregnancy.

ENGELS (*sighs wearily*): That's all it takes. Gott!

MARX: He can't help.

ENGELS: Who's the father? Not that little wanker, Schramm, is it?

MARX: You don't know?

ENGELS: My God! It's not you, is it?

MARX: I was about to ask you the same question.

ENGELS: You can't be serious?

MARX: Those long walks on Hampstead Heath, last Autumn?

ENGELS: Yes, but... (*deep sigh*) how many months?

MARX: Six.

ENGELS: Then there's nothing can be done. Is it you?

MARX: They'll all say it's me. Willich, Schapper. The émigré Deutsche scumbags, muck-raking nanny goats, natter, natter, natter. To hell with programme and party. 'Doktor Marx, servant-screwer, housemaid-humper, nanny-knocker.'

ENGELS: Would they be right, I wonder?

MARX: 'Right?' (*Pause.*) 'Right!' What are you talking about, 'right'? What the hell's 'right' got to do with it?

ENGELS: No lectures on class morality. I ask you as a friend.

MARX: Please, spare me the ethical metaphysics. I thought we were in a class struggle. I didn't know it was a competition in chastity. The working class wants Liberation, not masturbation. What's important is what the petty-bourgeois anarchist riff-raff will make of this, with their tiny little minds and their grubby little conspiracies.

ENGELS: Karl! Are you the father?

MARX (*pause*): My true heir has yet to be born. My brainchild! And when he is, he won't be conceived on a filthy mat in a Soho dungeon. The gestation period will take decades. The child will be fostered by millions, but the conception will be immaculate. (*With quiet ferocity.*) Anything, anything that stands in the way of that perspective is vile, immoral, irrelevant and insignificant. Without this book, the proletariat cannot begin to know itself. It's the final settlement with the present and its squalid past, the testament of the future.

ENGELS (*pause*): Then we need a noble lie!

They stand facing each other, eye to eye.

ENGELS: And who more noble than I?

Long silence.

ENGELS: Mohr! Fill up the glasses. (*MARX does so.*) I am about to become a father!

MARX (*smiles*): I can already see fatherly pride swelling up in you! (*Pats ENGELS' stomach.*)

ENGELS: Of course, Jenny will never speak to me again. Never has liked me.

MARX (*puts arm around him*): That's jealousy! She sees you as a rival for my affections. She's right, dear Fried-rich. Ours is a marriage of minds.

ENGELS: It won't do my reputation any good. Engels the womaniser!

MARX: And what shall we call the baby?

ENGELS: I rather fancy Ludwig, but Wolfgang's nice.

MARX: A boy then?

ENGELS (*feeling his stomach*): I can tell by the way he's kicking, he's a fighter; besides you're the specialist in girls.

MARX: A boy it is. I have a name! (*They raise glasses.*)

MARX: To Friedrich! Freddy for short.

ENGELS: A stroke of genius!

BOTH: 'To Freddy!'

MARX: And his middle name – Heinrich, after me!

ENGELS: Our first child! How exciting! I can get Mary to knit him some baby clothes. Ah! Mary!

MARX: She need never know. I'll see to that. The father's name need not be registered. All that matters is they think he's yours!

ENGELS: What about Lenchen?

MARX: She can't afford to keep herself. We'll get him fostered. The day he's born. Out of the house immediately!

ENGELS: The neighbours will know nothing. The children won't remember; the émigrés denied their gossip.

MARX: It's perfect!

ENGELS: He'll join the ranks of the proletariat.

MARX: And the movement will determine his future.

ENGELS: Just one thing – I never want him in my house.

MARX: Mine neither! (*Turns back on ENGELS.*)

ENGELS: Now, tell me the truth! Come on, old fellow.

MARX (*turns around, ignores question*): You know Fred, I think that you and I should give the Communist Manifesto another good fucking!

ENGELS is silent with disbelief.

Blackout.

Scene Seven – Abundance

MARX is scribbling. JENNY is preparing water and towels. A loud knock.

MARX: The doctor! He's early.

JENNY: He's right on time. Always is. (*Leaves to let him in.*)

MARX resumes scribbling.

DOCTOR (*entering with JENNY close behind*): Doesn't seem a year since I last called.

MARX: It isn't!

DOCTOR: Do you know, my last delivery, third set of twins this week. Yes, twin girls. Mind you, the others were boys, you know. I think. Now! (*Turning to JENNY.*) Fraulein Demuth, you hide your pregnancy well!

MARX: That is my wife!

DOCTOR: Fraulein Demuth is your wife?

MARX: No! This is my wife. (*Indicating JENNY.*) Fraulein Demuth is in...

DOCTOR: Your study! (*Offers hand to JENNY.*) Frau Marx, and how is, um, little, the baby?

JENNY: Franziska? She's fine, Doctor.

MARX signalling frantically to get him out of the room.

DOCTOR: Yes, girls are stronger you know.

MARX: The delivery ward (*indicating*) is in...

DOCTOR: Your study. Don't tell me, turn left, first door. I'm getting to know my way round. (*Exits to bedroom.*)

JENNY follows. MARX resumes writing and becomes intensely involved.

LENCHEN (*voice off*): Aaaah! (*Breathing convulsively.*)

MARX stops writing.

DOCTOR (*voice off*): Short breaths, short breaths.

LENCHEN (*voice off*): Is it time?

JENNY (*voice off*): Give me your hand, Lenchen!

MARX stands.

DOCTOR (*voice off*): Now, next time. The contractions are right.

Agitated breathing from LENCHEN.

DOCTOR (*voice off*): Now, push! Push!

JENNY (*voice off*): Push, Lenchen, push!

MARX sits, resumes writing. Cries of baby.

DOCTOR (*voice off*): It's a lovely boy.

MARX stops momentarily. Rubs his hands.

JENNY (*voice off*): A lovely baby boy. He's beautiful!

LENCHEN (*voice off*): Give him to me. I want him.

Baby cries, off stage.

JENNY (*enters*): Just like little Guido. Isn't it wonderful!

MARX embraces her, but his face betrays anguish.

LENCHEN (*voice off*): Can I kiss him, Doctor?

DOCTOR (*entering, drying hands*): You can do anything you want
with him, he's all yours. Forever!

LENCHEN cries with happiness.

MARX: Can I see him, Doctor?

DOCTOR (*shakes head*): She's tired. They always get tearful
afterwards. Isn't that right, Frau Marx?

JENNY breaks into tears.

DOCTOR: See what I mean? (*Picks up bag.*) Well I, er...

MARX: Here, two pounds wasn't it?

DOCTOR: Guineas.

MARX: It was pounds last time.

DOCTOR: Supply and demand.

MARX: Yes, yes. Here, thank you!

DOCTOR (*leaving*): Thank you! It's usually the, er, father who pays. Goodbye, er, Fraulein, er, goodbye. See you next year? A most productive household.

Fade.

Scene Eight – Expropriation

Next morning. LENCHEN is now on a mattress in the living room, baby swaddled beside her. Knock on door.

LENCHEN: Komm!

Enter SCHRAMM, sad, with flowers.

LENCHEN: Konrad! I'm so pleased to see you.

SCHRAMM proffers flowers.

LENCHEN: Oh Konrad! They're lovely. (*Jumps out of bed.*) I'll get some water.

SCHRAMM: Here, I'll do it. (*SCHRAMM fills beer mug with water from jug and puts roses in it.*) There! For a beautiful girl.

LENCHEN: Oh Konrad. Kiss your Lenchen.

SCHRAMM: Nein, nein.

LENCHEN: Please, for old times sake?

SCHRAMM (*sadly*): What's past is past.

LENCHEN: Do you want to hold the baby?

SCHRAMM: Nein.

LENCHEN: Don't be upset.

SCHRAMM: I hope you and the General will be very happy.

LENCHEN: Konrad, it's not like that.

SCHRAMM: Oh really!

LENCHEN: I want to be friends with you, always.

SCHRAMM: Huh. Then you can write to me.

LENCHEN: Write?

SCHRAMM: I'm going to America. They're all going to America, all the émigrés.

LENCHEN: No.

SCHRAMM: There are lots of good German girls in America.

LENCHEN: But there are no nice German boys in London.

SCHRAMM: Lots of them. Fools. Silly fools who don't know the meaning of life.

LENCHEN: I do love you, Konrad.

SCHRAMM: It looks like it, doesn't it?

Knock on door, enter ENGELS, uncomfortably.

LENCHEN: General!

SCHRAMM clicks heels, bows to LENCHEN, passes ENGELS,

looks him up and down scornfully, and exits.

ENGELS: What's the matter with him?

LENCHEN: Well at least he brought me flowers. What kind of a father are you?

ENGELS: I'm not any kind of father!

LENCHEN: Don't shout, people will hear.

ENGELS: It's all right. There's only me and Mohr. Jenny's taken the kids off to Ramsgate. Can I see the baby?

LENCHEN (*holds baby close*): No, you can't!

ENGELS: I must be mad. Schramm's not talking to me. You're hostile. Jenny hates my guts, and I didn't even get a good screw out of it!

LENCHEN: Quiet. You'll start him crying!

ENGELS: God! Married life! Who'd be a father?

Enter MARX.

ENGELS: Talk of the Devil!

MARX: General!

ENGELS: At least he's talking to me! My dear Mohr. Your wish is my command. I trust there are no more pregnancies that I don't know about?

MARX: Shut up, General.

MARX and ENGELS seated either side and above LENCHEN.

MARX: Now, the arrangements. We'll take the baby to the family in

114

Hackney. They will foster. He is to be called Friedrich Heinrich.

LENCHEN: But...

ENGELS: As to the financial arrangements, I will pay for his upkeep and education until the age of sixteen. My lawyer has been informed.

LENCHEN: And shall I see him?

ENGELS: Not at first. It's best for the child that he grows up in the belief that his foster parents are his true parents; it's less complicated.

LENCHEN: But what about me?

MARX: Later when the child is settled, you can visit him, as an aunt or some such.

LENCHEN: Some such?

MARX: It's safer that way. The true identity of the mother could lead to the discovery of the father.

LENCHEN: No. No. I won't allow it. And I don't want him called Friedrich, or Heinrich. These are your names, not my names.

ENGELS: It has to be.

MARX (*not harshly*): If you really want to keep him you can go back to Germany, bring him up alone, perhaps.

LENCHEN: I have not the means. (*Very upset.*) At least let him be called Demuth.

MARX: Later, when he's older.

ENGELS: It's best this way, Lenchen. He'll want for nothing.

LENCHEN: Except a mother and a father. No, I love him. I want

115

him.

MARX: If he stays here every German émigré will say 'This is the son of Karl Marx'.

LENCHEN: And what's so wrong with that?

MARX: Jenny would leave me, take the children. I suppose I could manage, somehow.

LENCHEN (*crying*): Oh God help me! (*Long silence.*) Take the baby!

MARX (*quietly, to ENGELS*): Take it, outside.

ENGELS takes the child and exits.

LENCHEN: No, no. What am I doing!

MARX: It will be well looked after.

LENCHEN: It! It? What do you mean 'it'? He!

MARX (*subdued*): It's upsetting for all of us. In a week or two you'll feel different.

LENCHEN: No. Everything has changed. I could have married. But not now. Nor ever have another child, save Freddy, and he's lost to me.

MARX: I'm sorry this has happened.

LENCHEN: It didn't 'happen', Charley. It was your, our, doing.

MARX (*strokes her hair*): Well, it was not what I had planned and hoped for. Take comfort in the thought that little Freddie's future will be bright.

LENCHEN (*with quiet strength*): The 'future', Charley, starts right here, right now. What we do now, or what we fail to do, makes it what it will be!

MARX (*with conviction*): You think I don't know that? That's precisely why he has to be adopted. There is something that I must do. And only I can do it!

LENCHEN: This isn't right!

MARX: Lenchen, ours is the morality that makes the future possible. History will judge what's right, what's wrong, and who, by making sacrifices, serves its purpose. We're making sacrifices. It's not the easy option. And it hurts. Now there's morality for you.

LENCHEN: I want to believe you, but if we can't take responsibility for our own child, what hope in hell is there for all the rest? He could grow up a thief, a tyrant, blood upon his hands. His fault? Or ours?

MARX: The cause is right, Lenchen.

LENCHEN: Oh yes. And then if he turned out a wrong one, I suppose you could say 'Not of my flesh. Mine was just the conception. My brainchild!'

MARX: Look how we live, Lenchen. This squalor, penury, ceaseless writing, meetings, struggles. Is this selfishness?

LENCHEN: Ten of us to change the world. Already duels, treachery and lies. Your desk, my scullery and Jenny's tears. It is a sort of indulgence!

MARX: You don't make a perfect world with perfect people. We're being tested out, forged in a crucible, like swords.

LENCHEN (*tearfully*): Oh Charley. I wish I had your strength and your belief.

MARX: Never leave us. I need you. Jenny needs you, and the Movement requires this. You hold us all together. I must go. There's work to do. If there's anything, anything at all you need...

LENCHEN (*shakes head. MARX departs*): Oh Freddie! Freddie!

Fade.

Scene Nine – The Conception

In this scene a desk is high on a pedestal left, with a series of steps, seven or eight, leading up to it. The seat behind the desk is bathed in red light, spotlighted. The room is transformed and glows with red light, perhaps even red banners draped all around. It is not the flat, but some abstract location out of time and space. MARX's hair is groomed to make his head appear godlike with a huge lion's mane, as he appears in Highgate Cemetery. JENNY is kneeling in the middle of the stage. MARX enters and slowly mounts the steps to his desk.

JENNY (*trance like*): Who is the father?

MARX: Who the son and who the Holy Spirit? Come. Pick up your paper and your pen. There's work to do.

JENNY does so and sits hunched uncomfortably on a stool below the bottom step. MARX walks around his desk thoughtfully, dictating. JENNY writes.

MARX: The wealth of capitalist societies presents itself as an immense accumulation of commodities, it's unit being a single commodity. Our investigation must begin therefore with the analysis of this single commodity...

JENNY: Sorry? 'The analysis of...?'

MARX (*patiently*): 'This single commodity.'

JENNY nods.

MARX: A commodity is, in the first place, an object, that, by its

118

properties, satisfies human wants of some sort...

JENNY: 'By its properties...?'

MARX: Satisfies human wants of some sort. The nature of such wants, whether for instance they spring from the stomach (*thoughtfully*) or from fancy, makes no difference. Neither are we concerned to know how the object satisfies...

JENNY: 'Neither are we concerned...?'

MARX: Come on Jenny! Please!

JENNY (*trance like*): 'How the object satisfies these wants...'

MARX: Right!

Enter LENCHEN right, with bucket and scrubbing brush. She begins to scrub the floor, on her hands and knees, so that the three figures on stage are at three different, contrasting, heights.

MARX: Whether directly as a means of subsistence, or indirectly as a means of production...

Freeze. Spotlight on MARX's head and shoulders on high, behind desk. Rest of stage gradually blacks out. JENNY lets out an agonizing cry of despair (pre-recorded). It is the cry of all who died and suffered for what Marx unleashed upon the world. LENCHEN joins in the cry, which becomes deafening as MARX's face fades away in a spotlight. Cut/dead.

Blackout.

The End.

DOWNTOWN PARADISE

('A Year to Life')

'For every act of kindness there is a punishment.'

A Play for Two Actors

Original Cast

Rachel Bloom - Amanda Hurwitz
a radical Jewish lawyer, aged 30's

James Wilson ⎫
a black convict, aged 30's ⎬ Richard C Sharp
Masked Intruder ⎭

Director - Sarah Esdaile

ACT ONE
Prologue – The Meaning of Adagio

A secure penthouse in Hong Kong, 1982. RACHEL wheels herself on, in a wheelchair, to front stage left, either in front of the stage curtain or with the set behind blacked out. A black shawl covers her legs and she wears heavily shaded glasses. She is in her fifties and appears world-weary and worn out, quite different to her dynamism in the rest of the play.

RACHEL: Is there such a thing as a tale without a moral? I used to have a smart-assed answer to that question. Not an answer, exactly, but pretty damned smart. I'd say 'Show me your morality and I'll tell you the value of your house.' Yes. I believed that... because... the world is so unjust! Well, it's true isn't it?

Don't ask me how I got involved in the sixties revolution. Why! With a background like mine I was lucky to get a visa for the Age of Aquarius. Would you believe – a comfortable middle-class family, four bedrooms, three square meals a day, two lawns back and front, and one Sabbath – on the wrong day of the week!

Childhood would have been nice, I guess. People seem to rate it. But when I was four years old, there was no sign of me changing sex, so my folks bought me a cello as a kind of punishment. For ten years I was doing solitary with Johann Sebastian Bach, and he deserved it.

Look, don't give me all that crap about the Protestant work ethic. Try the Jewish one and get back to me! My God! I was still wearing braces when I made my debut at the Hollywood Bowl. Elgar's cello concerto. Boy, could I play that piece now! But my fingers don't obey. What has to happen to you before you know the meaning of 'adagio'? Life, that's what! Anyways, I escaped and ran away to Law School. As an attorney, at least you get to talk to people. People need lawyers and you don't have to be pretty. I specialised in prison law, so my clients were always glad to see me. At last I felt wanted, needed. They appreciated me. Except for one guy! One very special guy. The guy who changed my life for ever. He taught me good. He taught me the one thing I had never understood. For every act of kindness, there is a punishment. *(She retrieves a bottle of tablets from beneath the shawl and gulps a couple down from the palm of her hand.)* These are for the pain. Physical pain you can live with; it's the spiritual pain I can't bear. I

123

guess they could cure that too, if I took enough of 'em. Oh, I think about that. Not a day goes by I don't consider that!

Fade.

Scene One – Uptight

Prison cell, Santanero, California, January 1970, twelve years earlier. JAMES is doing press-ups as a younger RACHEL strolls in and halts in front of the cell. She's impressed with his physique.

JAMES: Ninety-five... ninety-six... ninety-seven... ninety-eight... ninety-nine... one hundred!

He collapses, breathing heavily and recovering his breath. RACHEL enters the cell, dressed in the late sixties style of American radicals. She wears thigh-length boots and a miniskirt. Her hair is loose and her spectacles are dramatic, to enliven a fairly plain countenance. JAMES leaps to his feet and starts doing slow Japanese martial arts movements, with sudden bouts of fast movement and with much controlled breathing through the nose and guttural shouts. He possesses an inner calm, or at least he makes the effort to control inner tensions. Initially RACHEL walks in rather brusquely, checking the documents in her bag, but when she catches sight of JAMES, she takes a few steps backwards, in awe of his concentration and his physicality. But she is not ogling. JAMES is physically very fit and gives the impression of being self-composed, which gives him enormous sex appeal. He walks to the bed, dries his head and body with a towel. He sits cross-legged on the bed and picks up a book which he starts to scan. She seems uncertain of whether to butt in on his self-contained privacy. She has a natural nervousness, even though she is a highly competent, formidable lawyer. RACHEL clears her throat. JAMES continues reading.

RACHEL: If it's not a good time...?

JAMES (*still reading*): Time? What's that?

RACHEL: I could call back. It's only a three hour drive.

124

JAMES slowly inserts an envelope to keep his place in the book. Puts it down. Rises slowly. Walks to greet her, coolly. They shake hands.

JAMES: Mrs Bloom?

RACHEL: James Wilson. I've read your stuff – I'm honoured.

JAMES: Grab a seat. You handling Herbie Hamilton's appeal?

RACHEL: Right.

JAMES: Shot a cop. He's one dead nigger.

RACHEL: I don't think so.

JAMES (*scathing*): Oh. You don't think so, huh!

RACHEL: Herbie never stops talkin' about you. Earl Redmond says you're 'the most'!

JAMES: Hamilton and Redmond – they talk real good!

RACHEL: They admire you.

JAMES: No. They scared o' me.

RACHEL: President of the Black Provisionals? Scared? I don't get it.

JAMES: I'm smarter'n they are.

RACHEL: Oh? This is a competition? I thought we were all in the same team.

JAMES chuckles.

RACHEL: Am I missing out on the joke?

JAMES: What would a white woman know about oppression?

RACHEL: I'm Jewish.

125

JAMES: What would a Jew know about slavery?

RACHEL: Well now, let me see. (*Counts on fingers.*) There was Egypt, Babylon, the Romans...

JAMES: Hardly within living memory.

RACHEL: We don't forget easy.

JAMES: You're talkin' three thousand years.

RACHEL: You're just the new kids on the block. You've heard of Auschwitz?

JAMES: Sure I have. You heard of Mississippi?

RACHEL: But you're from Chicago – a little far north for cotton plantations?

JAMES: We moved to LA to save on heating.

RACHEL: And did you?

JAMES: Yes but the rents were higher. The landlord was...

RACHEL: Jewish?

JAMES: You got it.

RACHEL: So you wouldn't let you daughter marry one?

JAMES: You believe in immaculate conception?

RACHEL: I'm sorry, I guess prison does as much for your sex life as marriage does for mine.

JAMES: Almost a third of my life, I bin here.

RACHEL: Nine years, eleven months and twenty one days, but who's counting?

126

JAMES: Right. And six, six, man, in solitary. Two of those with the doors welded shut.

RACHEL: Welded?

JAMES: That's what I said.

RACHEL sighs with anger. Gets papers from bag.

JAMES: Let's see. For a hundred dollar hold-up. My share – fifty dollars. Five dollars a year! Shit man, ten cents week, and no green stamps!

RACHEL (*checks papers*): The sentence was 'a year to life'. Whatever happened to your accomplice?

JAMES: Paroled. Sold his black ass. Guy thinks he's 'free'. No way.

RACHEL: Paroled, that was when? Sixty-four?

JAMES: They say everybody remembers exactly where they were the day they shot Kennedy. That's true, you dig? I was right here. You jus' don' forgit things like that!

RACHEL: That was the day they released Holden.

JAMES: Pigs made him crawl to the gates on his hands and knees, dragging his bag along with his teeth. It's called the 'Great Society'!

RACHEL (*laid back, matter of fact, looking through the records*): Nine parole boards, nine rejections. On what was initially a one-year sentence!

JAMES: 'A year to life!' 'Course it din' help none – me leadin' a protest against conditions here.

RACHEL (*looking through papers*): Or holding a prison officer hostage?

JAMES: Din' hurt him, none. Jes' took all his money in a poker game. (*Looks right at her.*) Do you play poker?

RACHEL (*looks right back at him*): Played strip poker once. Still had all my clothes at the finish.

JAMES: Never cheat at poker. Creates baa-a-ad feelin'.

RACHEL: I don't need to. (*Staring game stops. She checks files, matter of fact.*) Quite a record! '61 and '62 – assaulting a prison guard; '63 – assaulting a prisoner; '64 – assaulting a prisoner and a guard; '68 – causing bodily harm to two prison guards. Two?

JAMES: Third one ran off. I couldn't git 'im.

RACHEL: Oh yuh and this one. (*Stares at him again.*) Possession of illegal substances?

JAMES: The two cases are not unconnected.

RACHEL: It better be good.

JAMES: Scene one. A cell in solitary. One lonely con – me – reciting a Malcolm X speech to the assembled silence. Enter three little pigs. 'We goin' search yo' cell boy' squeals pig one. 'Illicit substances' grunts the second little piggy. 'Illicit substances my ass!' says the con. 'Yeah. Yo' ass is where we goin' look, boy! Hands on the wall and take yo' pants off!' I was explaining the impossibility of that particular sequence of manoeuvres, when the third little piggy pulled down my pants and began to shove three ounces of dope wrapped in plastic up my ass, while the other two held me down. Over my shoulder, I explained 'It's supposed to be sniffed thro' the nose porky!'

RACHEL: So they called a medic, and waited.

JAMES: You got it, counsellor, but I kept 'em waiting. Di'n shit for two days.

RACHEL: Dirty bastards!

JAMES: No. They wore gloves. Pigs are fastidious about cleanliness.

RACHEL: And fingerprints. So what's the story?

JAMES: Mrs Bloom...

RACHEL: The name's Rachel.

JAMES: After the Watts riots, then the Tet offensive, black cons get to thinking, like, why we in Vietnam, black GI's fightin' little yellow guys? We got no quarrel with 'em. We worse off than they are, some parts.

RACHEL: A lot of white folks are asking the same questions.

JAMES: Oh yeah but it's a luxury of the mind for them. We're at the cutting edge here, woman. Cons reading history, philosophy!

RACHEL: A tough way to graduate.

JAMES: In the exercise yard, I advise 'em what to read next. I got a buddy in here, a real good brother, Johnny Silver. You wouldn't believe Johnny. Ain't nothin' pigs fear more than a wise'd up black con who's finally figured out why he's in here.

RACHEL (*checking files*): Yes, he led the protest with you. Then we get this District Court Inquiry?

JAMES: Inquiry! You kiddin'?

RACHEL (*gets up, walks around, report in hand, quoting*): Rave reviews! Santanero prison – 'conditions of shocking and debased nature', 'transgressing elementary concepts of human decency.'

JAMES (*laughs out loud*): For the pigs that's like winning an Oscar. If any of 'em ever read it.

RACHEL: 'A prisoner kept naked, in a dark, unventilated cell for a week.' Wasn't even allowed to wash. (*Throws report down, bored, with disgust.*)

JAMES (*indicates that it was him*): Listen, reports like that are part of the racket. White liberals and black Ministers o' religion read that stuff on a Sunday after church, say 'Thank the Lord, the watchdogs of our democracy are seeking out injustice within the system', and then they say grace and eat a li'l lunch. Protect me from liberals!

RACHEL: Mr Wilson...

JAMES: James!

RACHEL: Hey! Easy on the word 'liberal'! I wasn't born yesterday, James. For longer than you've served, I've been working to get people out!

JAMES: I wasn't referring to you.

RACHEL: Just don't make friends into enemies! Luther King was a liberal.

JAMES: Luther King was was no threat to nothing!

RACHEL: Why'd they kill him then?

JAMES: Oh c'mon! We live in different worlds. Why, I'll bet you and your husband have a nice li'l place you can escape to weekends.

RACHEL: Oh brother! Weekends we escape from each other.

JAMES: What's he do, your husband?

RACHEL: We're in the same line of work. Same firm.

JAMES: Two lawyers' pay cheques. That's good livin'!

RACHEL: We're a collective. Six of us. Demos, draft resistance, and drug cases only.

JAMES: All the same – big bucks, huh?

RACHEL: All fees go into a pool. Each takes what he needs.

JAMES: You mean you trust each other?

RACHEL: I do this work because it's necessary and I've got the legal education that allows me to. To be free, you've gotta do what's necessary. If you weren't in prison...

JAMES: If I weren't in prison I'd be dead by now.

RACHEL: How so?

JAMES: Never could accept the rules.

RACHEL: Which rules?

JAMES: All of 'em. At school, I used to skip classes. Skip church. Even skipped basketball. Some coach freak tol' me I had a great future. Basketball! Shit, man!

RACHEL: Didn't figure at synagogue, neither.

JAMES: I mean, to fuck with all of it. Social conditioning! White man's education, to keep us in line.

RACHEL: It's a whole lot better than ignorance.

JAMES: Well, I am totally alienated from all that 'constitutional reform' bullshit.

RACHEL: The Constitution is not bullshit. We fought wars for it. Still are.

JAMES: Look. You got me all wrong. I ain't no Luther King. That kind of thing jus' turns my stomach.

RACHEL: Don't you want to make your mark?

JAMES: What we talkin' 'bout here? TV? Rock stars? I don' wanna hear 'bout no cute li'l Jackson Five shakin' their hands to their ears; no Diana Ross; no Supremes...

RACHEL: You're really not into success, are you?

JAMES: And be a Joe Frazier boxing kangaroo? Maybe a Johnny Mathis crooner? (*Sings.*) 'Look at me. I'm as helpless as a kitten up a tree.' A kitten in a fuckin' tree, man!

RACHEL: No. It isn't 'you'.

JAMES: Oh yeah and a-a-a-athletics! Me in my runnin' vest in the long jump pit, winnin' medals for Uncle Sam, when the white man fires the startin' pistol.

RACHEL: Now let's not get ambitious. It would ruin your image.

JAMES (*angrily*): I ain't one of them 'Frisco dudes with flowers in their hair. They jus' want a bridge over troubled waters while they row the boat ashore with Michael. Ain't no panther in 'em. They just tame tom-cats straight from the vet with their balls snipped.

RACHEL (*preparing to go*): Well Mr Wilson your plans for a life of obscurity are well in place. You obviously don't need my services. Here's my card if you change your mind.

Fade.

Scene Two – Pact

Prison cell, Santanero, March 1970. RACHEL has returned at JAMES' request.

RACHEL: I got your letter.

JAMES: Ain't been no change of heart on my part, but I like the way you operate. You still got illusions in the system but...

RACHEL: James, I'm real busy right now.

JAMES: What I mean is, I think you're on the level.

RACHEL (*tolerantly*): What do I get, a gold star?

JAMES: I think you could do me a lot of good.

RACHEL: Affirmative.

JAMES: There'd be somethin' in it fer you, too.

RACHEL: Let's not worry about that.

JAMES: OK. But I still figure the only way to get me out is to change the system that put me here.

RACHEL: Getting you out and changing the system are two sides of the same coin.

JAMES: I'm a revolutionary. Not a lawyer.

RACHEL: Thomas Jefferson was a revolutionary and a lawyer.

JAMES: Thomas Jefferson was a white slave owner! Used to screw his women slaves.

RACHEL: Revolutionaries are allowed to fuck, aren't they?

JAMES: If I ever get out of here, it won't be crawling on my hands and knees like Stevie Holden. I'll come out fighting 'til the whole rotten system is destroyed.

RACHEL: I'll go along with that.

JAMES: But can you go the distance? Don't mess with me unless you can.

RACHEL: It's not a question of distance, it's a question of objectives. I share your objectives.

JAMES: You share?

RACHEL: I'm a lawyer, working against the system from within the system.

JAMES (*laughs*): And you believe that's possible, without armed force?

RACHEL: Just watch me.

JAMES: Just watch. That all? Where do I figure?

RACHEL: You'll be so busy, there won't be enough hours in the day.

JAMES: Time I've got plenty of.

RACHEL: But if you are to be my client...

JAMES: Your client?

RACHEL: Yes. We've got to do this my way. You have to be advised by me. You have to trust me.

JAMES: Shit! I never trusted no one in ma whole life!

RACHEL: Well, do you?

JAMES: Do I what?

RACHEL: Trust me.

JAMES: That's a toughie. Anyone who thinks they can get me out of here, except in a coffin, has to be crazy. Either they don't understand the system, or they don't understand me. Should I trust a crazy person? (*Chuckles.*) But yeah, I trust you, you crazy bitch! Git me outa here!

RACHEL: I take it you have engaged my services?

JAMES: I don't have no money.

RACHEL: When I get to work on this case, the money will come flooding in, James, flooding in!

JAMES: Like, from where?

RACHEL: There's a lot of good, decent, honest folk out there who just haven't been told the truth. We're gonna tell it like it is.

JAMES: And what about you? Do you trust me?

RACHEL: If I didn't, I wouldn't be here. (*Walks.*) I don't like the way this country's moving. The White House is like a sealed fortress these days. You know what separates the politicians from the criminals? They do it legally.

JAMES: Right on baby! We're the future, cons from the ghettos.

RACHEL: James. I know about ghettos. My grandparents lived in one.

JAMES: But I'm different. I'm a mean mother. The other cons are scared o' me. I'm a theoretician who kicks my enemy when he's down. Cons fear me. Pigs too!

RACHEL: I'm scared of you!

JAMES: You'd trust someone you're scared of?

RACHEL nods.

JAMES: Trust, really trust? You wouldn't weaken if the pigs framed me? Spread lies about me and Johnny Silver?

RACHEL: Know what they call me?

JAMES: 'Attorney of the last resort.'

RACHEL: If I wanted easy cases, I'd know where to find 'em.

JAMES: You feel sorry for me, don't you?

RACHEL: Absolutely not!

JAMES: You tryin' to prove something to yourself.

RACHEL: No.

JAMES: That you ain't no racist.

RACHEL: I'll ignore that.

JAMES: Ever known a white girl sleep with a black guy just to prove somethin' to her friends?

RACHEL: Isn't it just awful that you can even think something like that?

JAMES: So. Why you takin' this case? You don't know the real me.

RACHEL: Please, don't ask me that.

JAMES: I'm trouble. Big trouble.

RACHEL: You've never killed a man.

JAMES: But I've wanted to.

RACHEL: But you didn't.

JAMES: I could name a few who're jus' askin' for it!

RACHEL: I've gotten people off homicide charges.

JAMES: Were they innocent?

RACHEL: I guessed they were.

JAMES: But you didn't know for sure.

RACHEL: As sure as I needed to be.

JAMES: Did you ask them, straight?

RACHEL: In one case, yes.

JAMES: And?

RACHEL: That's a professional confidence. I'd rather not talk about it.

JAMES: You know what you're dealing with? There are cons in here who'd slit their own grandmothers' throats to gain a few privileges.

RACHEL: If a man is goaded, he's gonna strike out to preserve his status as a human being. I can live with that. Condone it, even.

JAMES: In here, pigs rule by turning cons against each other; whites against blacks; blacks against chicanos; blacks against other blacks and not-so-blacks. Pigs need rats.

RACHEL: Seems that way.

JAMES: In here, nothing is what it seems. Nobody is who or what they seem. If a con gets killed, no way anybody will ever know the truth of his guilt or innocence. It's a corridor of revolving mirrors in a fog. Ain't no truth 'bout nothing.

RACHEL: There is a truth but we have to fight for it. We have to make truth.

JAMES: Well I'm relieved to hear that.

RACHEL: Otherwise James, what's the point of anything?

JAMES: Remember this. If I should die in here, some pig even, they'd just blame any con they want to be rid of. The pigs would conspire with the guilty con to nail the guy they want, and then they'd figure ways to get the guilty con put down. Machiavelli wouldn't last a minute in here.

RACHEL: The phrase is 'beyond reasonable doubt'.

JAMES: Cock-suck it – no! In here it's 'beyond unreasonable doubt!'

RACHEL: Well at Santanero prison, the boundaries of reasonable doubt would require some logical extension.

JAMES: Right! To survive in here a con has to think like a pig, has to be more devious than a pig. And a pig is devious to the power of 'F'!

RACHEL: But you've survived.

JAMES: Yuh. But for what? This ain't a life. Sometimes, I feel... ah shit!

RACHEL: Don't be ashamed to say it.

JAMES: Warmth, closeness. I guess it's a weakness.

RACHEL: No it isn't. You deserve it. (*She goes as if to lay a hand on his shoulder. He pulls away.*) I don't know if this is any help to you, but there is something which I believe in very strongly.

JAMES: Don' hit me with the God crap. I was jus' gettin' to like you.

RACHEL: I gave up on him some time ago.

JAMES: Well he's sure got a lot to answer for. No forgiveness for that mother!

RACHEL: You know, fighting a common cause brings people together like nothing else. Makes us different people. Makes relationships clean and honest.

JAMES: All I have is faith in myself and what I believe.

RACHEL: It doesn't have to be that way.

JAMES: Most people don't measure up.

RACHEL: You're asking an awful lot.

JAMES: Yes. I am.

A bell rings.

RACHEL: My time's up.

JAMES: Now hear this! Don't take me on unless it's all the way.

RACHEL: I made my decision before I came here. Before I even knew the details. (*Conspiratorially.*) Here put these on! (*Hands him some horn-rimmed spectacles.*)

JAMES: Hell, I don't need glasses.

RACHEL: You do so! Stand in front of the bars. Don't look happy. Don't look sad. Be proud.

JAMES: I am proud. (*He poses. She snaps him with prison bars in the background and slips camera back in bag.*)

RACHEL: Day one on the road to freedom! (*Makes a fist. He returns it, thoughtful. She exits.*)

JAMES (*chuckles, takes glasses off, throws them on the bed*): Shit, man! Wow! (*He starts to sing an old Negro spiritual, but with derision.*) 'Oh happy day... Wooooohoa! Oh happy day! When Jes-us wa-a-alks...' Yeah! (*Laughs, cynically. He resumes his martial arts routine, purposefully.*)

Fade.

Scene Three – Set-back

Prison cell, Santanero, later.

RACHEL: Just hold my hand a while. (*He clasps her hand.*) All the time, I was thinking about you. (*Places her other hand over his.*)

JAMES: Me?

RACHEL (*nods*): You all right?

JAMES *nods.*

RACHEL: Good to see you.

JAMES: You too.

RACHEL: D'they treat you bad?

JAMES: I can handle it.

RACHEL: I don't know how...

JAMES: Lots of practice...

RACHEL: I've never met anyone like you. I thought Herbie was strong...

JAMES: The hotter the furnace, the tougher the steel.

RACHEL: But how...

JAMES: I'm alive! That's what I keep reminding myself. They killed Johnny Silver and Lou Stevens, but they made a mistake by not killing me. I feel no emotion, no pain – jus' proud flesh.

RACHEL: You must feel something.

JAMES: Sentiment is a weakness. Eats you up inside. Makes you a victim.

RACHEL: I went to see your mother...

JAMES: Why'd you do that?

RACHEL: I jus' thought... I needed...

JAMES: I don' wanna hear 'bout family. That's a false world. In here you see things clear. This is how it is. This is America.

RACHEL: Why Johnny? Why Lou?

JAMES: They black ain't they?

RACHEL: Prosecution says it was a race fight.

JAMES: Sure it was. But it was fixed.

RACHEL (*opening a file and reading*): 'A' wing – the exercise yard...

JAMES: Seven blacks. Twelve hand-picked whites, who'd probably be expelled from the Klan for racism. Pigs placin' bets on who'll win. The rednecks make like monkeys, scratch their armpits. Johnny gives the black power salute and they kick him to the ground. Lou and the other five brothers wade in to rescue him. Two shots from a tower guard. And it's all over.

RACHEL (*still reading through files*): No white casualties.

JAMES: The guard is a marksman, right! What he aims for he hits.

RACHEL (*throwing down file in disgust. She rises, walks around*): Even though it's like a pile of guys in a football game... two black bull's-eyes!

JAMES (*following her*): No warning on the public address! Johnny's already dead. Louey's on the deck, bleeding to death. Then a pig shouts 'Freeze!' The hospital wing is right close by. Louey lies there groaning for twenty minutes! Black cons can't help him or they're dead too. It's half an hour before Louey gets attention – too late!

RACHEL (*distressed*): Who organised the hunger strike?

JAMES: Organise? Hell, it don' need no organisin'! First degree murder kinda puts guys off their food – even white cons empty their mess tins on the floor.

RACHEL: Jesus Christ, 'justifiable homicide!' What was the D.A. thinking about?!

JAMES: His ass!

RACHEL: But he recommended the verdict before the grand jury even convened!

JAMES: 'Grand jury!' How many blacks on it?

RACHEL: Not one.

JAMES: Ain't that jus' grand!

RACHEL: And no black was permitted to testify!

JAMES: Goddammit! I tell you when that verdict comes over the radio, this place just explodes. It's like the souls of the damned rattling the gates of hell...

Sound of bars being hit with metal.

JAMES: It starts in the corner of a distant wing and picks up speed along the walkways like a gathering hurricane. Pigs running up and down the aisles of tiers one and two, smashing their sticks against hands and fingers.

RACHEL: Officer Steiger's death – did you see it personally?

JAMES: I wish I had. But in my dreams I see that mother's eyes pop from their sockets. I see the long fall. It's a slo-mo replay. I see his body hit each steel handrail on each floor, ricochet and spin like space-junk in the outer darkness. And then, oh joy, I see his frail skull crumple like an eggshell as his small brains slip out through the crack across the polished floor like a grey yolk.

RACHEL: God Almighty! This place!

JAMES: Fuck Steiger! One less pig! Think of Johnny. Think of Louey.

RACHEL: Revenge is not a legal defence. Let's stay with Officer Steiger. Tell me what you know.

JAMES: Ain't nothin' to tell.

RACHEL: You know who did it, don't you?

JAMES is silent.

RACHEL: And you're not going to say?

JAMES shakes head.

RACHEL: Why protect them? The prison authorities are pinning it on you!

JAMES: You sound surprised, counsellor.

RACHEL: It's a mandatory death sentence under section 4500!

JAMES: Why I tol' you woman – they tryin'a kill me!

RACHEL: Keep silent – and they do it legally!

JAMES: That's between them and whatever devil they pray to!

RACHEL: I understand your code of honour, but...

JAMES: To fuck with 'honour!' It's not 'honour', I'm not going to rat.

Uneasy pause.

RACHEL: What happened, dammit? I wanna know what happened!

JAMES: You read the transcript?

RACHEL: It points to you and Oscar Watts. Was Watts involved?

JAMES: Next cell to mine. He's political, like me.

RACHEL: Was he involved?

JAMES: Ask him!

RACHEL: I've drafted in another lawyer to help on his case. Friend of mine. One of the best.

JAMES: We don't deserve you, baby.

RACHEL: Keep talking.

JAMES: Well, after Steiger hits the concrete – pig invasion of 'B' wing. All of us on tier three are 'interrogated', which is kinda euphemism fo' squash rackets – small room with a nigger for a ball. I was in so much pain from my ribs I thought I would suffocate. My balls swelled up like balloons. After that, solitary was a blessing....

In the following sequence, they move about the stage 'blocking' and reconstructing the incident as if in a courtroom.

RACHEL: Wait. Where exactly are you in 'B' wing when it happens?

JAMES: Like I say, tier three...

RACHEL: Which is where Steiger falls from, and all the prisoners on that tier are standing outside their cells, waiting to be locked in?

JAMES: No. Some are still making their way up the stairwell at the far end.

RACHEL: And where are you?

JAMES: In my cell.

RACHEL: Door open?

JAMES: Door open.

RACHEL: And Watts?

JAMES: The cell wall obstructs my line of vision. Oscar could be in or out.

RACHEL: Which do you think?

JAMES: Can't say for sure.

RACHEL: And where's Steiger?

JAMES: Just beyond my cell, last on the tier, by the down stairway. It's one-way.

RACHEL: Can you see if Oscar runs past your cell?

JAMES: The disturbance is on the other side.

RACHEL: Opposite? Or to your left?

JAMES: My left.

RACHEL: Yes, of course. So you must have seen Steiger run past your cell?

JAMES: No. My back was to him. Din' see him. I heard him.

RACHEL: And then?

JAMES: A commotion. Some guy's takin' punishment.

RACHEL: Steiger? Or a con?

JAMES: Con mos' likely. By the time I step outside, Steiger's dead meat, three floor down. Cons runnin' everywhere, mostly to their cells.

RACHEL: And Watts?

JAMES: Oscar's by the door of his cell.

RACHEL (*gets up, walks*): Three prosecution eye-witnesses swear you and Watts pushed him over.

JAMES: Black or white?

RACHEL: All black.

JAMES: So who are they?

RACHEL: At the request of the prosecution, the judge refuses to divulge the names.

JAMES: On what grounds?

RACHEL: On the grounds that inmate witnesses could be attacked by other inmates.

JAMES: Damn right, they would!

RACHEL: My guess is they've all been moved to other prisons to make life difficult for the defence. We're fighting that ruling. We have to know those names!

JAMES: Find them and you've got your men.

RACHEL: Once we know, we'll discredit them.

JAMES: Discredit! Hell, most of them are in for rape or manslaughter anyhows.

RACHEL: I'm workin' on it. Did you know they got the builders in, restructuring tier three, destroying evidence?

JAMES: It's hopeless. They want me and nothin's gonna stop 'em!

RACHEL: Don't ever say that! Hear me? Don't even think it!

JAMES: While you are planning my defence thro' due process, the prison authorities are workin' on the frame up. You made one big mistake Rachel. You believe in the law. But they don't!

Fade.

Scene Four – Making it

Prison cell, Santanero, later. RACHEL in mid-conversation, having just arrived. She puts down her handbag.

RACHEL: I've filed a motion for the removal of Judge Bradshaw from your case.

JAMES: You've what?

RACHEL: There's a design fault in every lie. We traced statements of the learned judge that would make even Goebbels blush!

JAMES: You never give up, do you? What are the chances?

RACHEL: Even money – he stands down this week. We're also challenging the grand jury judgements on the grounds of its racial composition.

JAMES: White as the driven snow!

RACHEL: Next thing is the state legislators' report on conditions right here in Santanero, also due this week. I have it on good authority that's it's absolutely damning.

JAMES: You're kiddin' me.

RACHEL: Then we'll get you moved out of Santanero, to a place where you stand the chance of a fair trial.

JAMES: Jesus! Where you comin' from?

RACHEL: Well sure as hell not from Jesus. I believe in you James. I believe in you more than you believe in yourself. Because this case is bigger than any one person. You are the embodiment of a cause that started with the Civil War, and that cause is beyond questioning.

JAMES: Hey! Wait, wait, wait. It's my life at stake here. I'm the one on trial.

RACHEL: You really believe that? You really believe that you are on trial?

JAMES: Yeah. I figure that my ass is on the line.

RACHEL: Well you're wrong, James. You are not on trial because the system is in a criminal conspiracy against you, and I will prove that in court by due process. The 'evidence', unquote, against you has been concocted by convicted criminals and prison guards, whose prison is about to be condemned as the Dachau of America, by a grand jury of Imperial Wizards and a judge who is a self-confessed racist. We're gonna stand this trial on its head. They are the defendants. We are the prosecutors. We are indicting the police and the prison authorities. We are indicting the grand jury and the Courts. We are indicting the judge and the media. The system is on trial. I'm doing it right now with Herbie Hamilton's appeal. I'll get Hamilton off. We'll win the appeal. Get it straight in your head. You're gonna walk free!

JAMES: My God. You're unbelievable!

RACHEL: OK?

JAMES: OK.

RACHEL: We're going to shift the entire focus of this trial away from the details of the charges against you. That's the only way we can win. This case is beyond 'right' and 'wrong'. It's a cause that creates it's own ethics.

JAMES: I do believe you're serious.

RACHEL: Take a look at this. (*Hands over a paper.*) The names of yours and Oscar's defence committee – academics, scientists, psychologists, poets. You name them, we've signed them up.

JAMES: You did all this before you took me on, didn't you?

RACHEL: They believe in you, too. All-American men and women of international standing. (*Takes a wad of papers from file. Hands to him.*)

JAMES (*reading it*): 'An appeal to the conscience of America... against legalised murder...'

RACHEL: The Defence Fund has just been launched. I'll update you on the total. I shan't use a cent without your authorisation.

JAMES: I don't know what to say.

RACHEL: You don't have to 'say' anything. But you do have to write a little more. Take a look through the papers.

JAMES: Where d'you get these?

RACHEL: That's why I had to go visit your mother.

JAMES: My letters to my family.

RACHEL: We're publishing! I made a selection.

JAMES: Why a selection?

RACHEL: Some are, perhaps a little repetitive. Some just unsuitable, I guess.

JAMES: In what way 'unsuitable'?

RACHEL: It's your decision, of course. They're your letters.

JAMES: Why 'unsuitable'?

RACHEL: You write some very harsh things about your mother and father.

JAMES: You should hear what they say about me. That I failed 'em. That I was always the baddest. Why they even prayin' for me.

RACHEL: James, my folks are just the same. My mother still hopes for me to take up property law. 'Respectable, with a regular practice!'

JAMES: Shit. I checked out the alias files on her lilywhite, western God and told her – he's a hit-man for the WASP mafia.

RACHEL: And you wonder why she gets mad?

JAMES: The system's done a zero-resistance job on my momma – on her knees every Sunday, prayin' for her skin to turn a lighter shade of pale.

RACHEL: James, so much depends on this book. We've got to get it right. They need the proofs for the end of the month.

JAMES: My momma failed me! My poppa moonlights to fill the church
collection bowl. Now you want me to kiss-ass at the do-gooders convention?

RACHEL (amused): I wouldn't put it like that, even if I could!

JAMES: Well what then?

RACHEL: Tell the truth as you see it, but...

JAMES: But what?

RACHEL: Be magnanimous to those who love you. Understand, their motives are the finest, even though you don't go along.

JAMES: So. James Wilson is to be packaged as clean-assed merchandise for white opinion. That what you're sayin?

RACHEL: I'm saying this book could turn it all around for you. You don't have to compromise with any part of the system, and I wouldn't want you to. We'll include some of your views on history and economics. You've worked it all out, no formal education – an original voice!

JAMES: You're not so bad yourself, firebrand. Ain't much of you, but you fill all the spaces. Where'd you get it from?

RACHEL: Me?

JAMES: Yeah. You're one of us!

RACHEL: Don't say that.

JAMES: Why not?

RACHEL: Because it's not true. I wish I were.

JAMES: What are you then, Rachel Bloom?

RACHEL: Oh, I don't know. A disciple, I guess.

JAMES: Daniel's disciple, who leads from behind.

RACHEL: I don't, do I?

JAMES: Aw, come on! You got this whole thing figured – the defence, the committee, the campaign, the book, the publicity. Why I'm just putty in your hands, disciple! You runnin' the whole show.

RACHEL: I'm not. I'm really not. I just happen to be on the outside where I can get things done. In fact, I've always been an outsider. I just want to belong.

JAMES: You're doin' a swell job. I'm not sure why you're so devoted, but I sure appreciate it. I'm a difficult mother but you, you're just as contrary. That's why we get along. Besides, ain't never had a disciple before.

RACHEL: I don't know whether I ought to say this...

JAMES: Say it.

RACHEL: This thing's taken over my whole life, like there's nothing else.

JAMES: Somethin' wrong with that?

RACHEL: I'm not sure I want it to, and yet there's another part of me says yes, yes, yes, let it happen!

JAMES: What does your husband think?

RACHEL: Yuh, well...

JAMES: You've gone awful quiet.

RACHEL: Have I?

JAMES: Things all right between you?

RACHEL nods.

JAMES: If he respects you, he should support you in what you want.

RACHEL: Oh, he does. That's the problem. Sometimes I wish he'd slap me. Tell me to wise up. Always so calm and quiet. Figures I get too involved in my cases.

JAMES: Yuh?

RACHEL: Well, Nathan says a good lawyer should always keep a distance. He's worried.

JAMES: What the hell about?

RACHEL (*close to tears; emotional*): He's worried it will... destroy me.

JAMES: If it ain't worth dyin' for, it ain't worth doin'.

RACHEL: Nobody's ever put it into words for me before.

JAMES: So. You are vulnerable, after all?

RACHEL: I'm so scared, I'm shaking. Nathan wants to split.

JAMES: Ain't nothing to be scared of.

RACHEL: He's right. It will destroy me.

JAMES: I won't let that happen. I care about you too.

RACHEL: I dash around organising, speech-making, I addressed a campus meeting last week and everybody thinks I'm strong, in charge of things. Yet inside, I feel just like a prisoner. (*Sinks head in hands.*)

JAMES: Well, if that's the way you feel, maybe you should keep your professional distance. Don't get involved with me on a personal level.

RACHEL: It's too late, James. I am. More than I want to be. And that's the truth.

JAMES: Well I'll tell you somethin' to make you change your mind. You've been level with me and I'm going to do the same with you.

RACHEL: You don't have to.

JAMES: In here, the sexual frustrations are explosive. Guys jack-off over fuck-mags, do tricks for pink-ass pigs or generally suck around.

RACHEL: I don't want to hear.

JAMES (*quietly in the gloom, almost seductively*): They get gut-flutters for the new boys. Shower time's an orgy. No small talk. Gang-shags for pretty shitbirds. If they fight it, they get suffocated, and gasp for air, just like an orgasm.

RACHEL: Oh God, really, please...

JAMES: You just want to hug the poor bastard who's been raped, but you can't be sure why. Back in your cell, you fantasise about him and jack off, cos you couldn't sink to takin' him. When I was a rookie, they tried me out. I sank my teeth into the nearest dick and held on like a pit-bull. They never tried again. That's my only sexual experience since conviction. Not exactly romance. Nearest I got to 'intimacy' in ten whole years. I mean this Rachel. You're the best friend I ever had.

RACHEL: Is that all?

JAMES: I don't want to spoil it all. Don't want to hurt you.

RACHEL: I knew the first time we met, but I'm not pretty, so...

JAMES: You're beautiful. Put your arms around me.

RACHEL is resigned to what follows. Puts arms around him, a little nervously. JAMES kisses her long and turns her till her back is against the wall. She stands submissively and he sinks to his knees, raising her dress and kissing her thighs as she runs her fingers through his hair. Not much can be seen, but her breathing is audible. JAMES pulls down her panties and she steps out of them a little clumsily and embarrassed. Throws her arms around him, kissing. He lifts her up against the wall. They couple and make love frantically, JAMES with his back to the audience. There is a loud banging on the door and the sound of keys being turned.

Blackout.

Interval.

ACT TWO
Scene One – High

Prison cell, San Felipe, Califonia, June 1970.

RACHEL: They're running scared!

JAMES (*singing*): 'Heard it on the grapevine...'

RACHEL (*joins him in a duet*): 'Jus' about to lo-o-se mah mind, honey honey!' (*She embraces JAMES, but he's never as demonstrative about such contact.*)

RACHEL: Me oh my! Just love your new place! Mm-mmh! Movin' up in the world!

JAMES: Bijou, baby! Bijou. Property's expensive here in San Felipe! My interior designer is planning an extension! (*Snaps out of it.*) So, you did it for Herbie.

RACHEL: We sure did.

JAMES: But he was guilty as hell.

RACHEL: Not according to the law.

JAMES: Then the law is an asshole!

RACHEL: Trampled on their own procedures, and paid the price. Oh, oh. Almost forgot. (*She gets two copies of his newly published book from her case.*) Your book! One for you, and one for me.

JAMES (*holds it in his hands like gold, strokes the cover with his hand*): Now, I'm immortal.

RACHEL: Happy with it? Took a lot of editing. What do I get? (*Sticks out her cheek, posily, for a kiss.*)

JAMES: What can I say? You're the most... how's it doin'?

RACHEL: Sell out – first day! They're reprinting. Here. (*From bag.*) You want reviews? Reviews! Read, enjoy!

JAMES (*reading aloud from clippings*): 'James Wilson, awaiting trial for the alleged murder of prison guard Frederick Steiger...' what's with the 'Frederick'? Pig's name was Steiger.

RACHEL: Read on.

JAMES: 'His style is unique. A streetwise philosopher and with a language that is direct, challenging, at times, almost poetic.'

RACHEL: And this, listen, from the Tribune: 'Most fascinating are Wilson's chapters on 'Politics – the Art of the Impossible...' and so they go on.

JAMES: Let me see. (*Takes it from her.*) 'That said – the book is curiously silent on solutions....' This guy hasn't even read it.

RACHEL: That's not important, but this is: 'Wilson, one time dime-store hold-up artist, has triumphed over his past to become a prophet...'

JAMES: Couldn't have put it better myself!

RACHEL: Author! Author! (*Claps him.*) Would you sign my copy, sir?

JAMES (*sits on table, takes a pen*): Stand back there. Give a guy some room, you'll all be served!

RACHEL: A dedication. (*Dictates.*) 'To Rachel Bloom – diplomatic representative of the Black Provisional Government...'

JAMES: Hold it! Hold it! Who's the writer 'round here? How's about 'To Rachel, friend, disciple and loyal lieutenant?!'

RACHEL: How's about... 'lover'?

JAMES: Stand in line. All requests for sex will be considered

156

impartially and without prejudice!

RACHEL: James, we've done it. This trial is decided before we walk up the steps of the courthouse.

JAMES: Sock it to me!

RACHEL (*gets poster from bag and hides it behind her back, teasing*): Now, guess whose picture is on every student's wall on campuses, coast to coast?

JAMES: Gimme that!

RACHEL (*runs around, playfully*): No. No. You can't. Guess!

JAMES corners her.

RACHEL (*kisses him. He responds but less enthusiastically. She whispers*): Oh... oh... on the bed. I want you.

JAMES (*whispers*): It's risky right now. Besides, I'd hate to spoil my chances with my campus chick fan club.

RACHEL (*whispers*): I've got a low climax threshold. Twenty seconds to jackpot.

JAMES: Give me the poster first.

RACHEL gives him the poster.

JAMES (*unfurls it*): This is the shot you took, right?

RACHEL: Cute, isn't it? You look so sad.

JAMES tacks it on the wall.

RACHEL: Glasses do it for you. A tragic hero.

JAMES: Tragic, my ass! Defiant, accusing, awesome!

RACHEL: You are now a campus icon. Pleased?

JAMES: What's an icon?

RACHEL: A Russian holy picture. A saint.

JAMES: No shit?

RACHEL Saint James!

JAMES: How's about – an avenging angel? I like that better.

RACHEL: Avenging angel. You got it! James, I have to tell you, the Collective is swamped out with groupie letters.

JAMES: Do I get to answer them personally?

RACHEL (*shakes her head*): We sent out circulars, thanking them, with a tear off slip to join the support groups. Oh, and you got the usual: three pairs of panties.

JAMES (*inhales loudly*): Mail 'em to me!

RACHEL: Last week, a civil rights march in Chicago. The Defence Committee had the biggest contingent. They were all carrying that poster.

JAMES: Get me a guitar, we'll press an album!

RACHEL: Do you get to see TV newscasts?

JAMES: Hell no! Presley movies, Bilko and the fuckin' Flintstones. Three hundred cons – fist fights over channel hopping.

RACHEL: Last week, clips from 'Free Wilson' demos all over Europe. Listen, there was even one in Wales.

JAMES: Wales? Not on my file.

RACHEL: Wales, England, right? And there were questions in the

Italian Congress.

JAMES: Italian Congress? I din' know they had a government!

RACHEL: Out there, it's like a great seismic shudder of what's coming. I've gotten so many invites to campus meetings, I've got to ration my appearances.

JAMES: So you're also a celebrity?

RACHEL: On TV chat shows, I have to weigh my words carefully. The prosecution's waiting, waiting for me to make one slip and screw it all up. Three hours sleep a night, if I'm lucky.

JAMES: What does Nathan Bloom make of all this?

RACHEL (*pauses for a moment*): Nathan and I have split.

JAMES: Oh. I'm sorry to hear that. Is there, someone else?

RACHEL: A broad, hovering in the wings. Always had the hots for him.

JAMES: I don't figure in this, do I? Ain't no home-breaker.

RACHEL: Ours is a home of the mind – the movement. I don't care about material things anymore.

JAMES: Did you move out?

RACHEL: No. Nathan did. I think he suspects.

JAMES: About?

RACHEL: Us!

JAMES: Woah! Woah! Hold on. It's early days.

RACHEL: Yeah. Early days. There'll be a lot more. Better ones. Six months on – freedom, a new life. All to play for.

JAMES: You got a crush on me?

RACHEL: Think about you every day. You're becoming my life.

JAMES: Easy, easy. I'm real fond of you. Think about you, too.

RACHEL: Well then...

JAMES: Let's just, leave it open. See how things develop. I don't rule anything out.

RACHEL: You don't?

JAMES: I owe you so much!

RACHEL: What's to 'owe'? We're in this together.

JAMES: But I've never had a life, Rachel. This is all I know. This whole affair is unreal. I need time.

RACHEL: You're right. I'm being selfish. Forgive me. Kiss me.

JAMES (*turns his back, holds temples*): Cool it, will ya. Jus', you know. Chrissakes, I'm under sentence of death.

RACHEL (*still pursuing him, touching*): I'm sorry. I shouldn't... I didn't mean...

JAMES: All right. All right.

RACHEL (*again embracing him from behind*): It's gonna be OK. Everything's gonna work out.

JAMES (*sighs, disentangles*): Yuh, yuh!

RACHEL: The Feds are real attentive right now.

JAMES: The Feds?

RACHEL: There's a car parked outside my house twenty-four hours.

At two in the morning, I peep through the curtains. There they are. When I do rallies there's always some guy with a tape recorder.

JAMES: I'll make a revolutionary out of you yet.

RACHEL: Sometimes, walking home, I get kinda scared, look for someone to shout to. Emptiness comes back at me.

JAMES: At the end of the day, each of us is alone.

RACHEL: It's natural. They should be curious. I'm on TV more times than Liberace.

JAMES: You getting fan mail, too?

RACHEL: I'm a one-man woman.

JAMES: Come on, Rachel. I'm winding you up! Come here, disciple. Wanna do it now?

RACHEL (*turns away*): I've gone off the boil a li'l.

JAMES: Women!

RACHEL: The trial's shaping up for September sometime. By the way, we got the names of those witnesses. Tapes of the evidence.

JAMES: What's the verdict?

RACHEL: We could march the entire marine corps through the middle of it. One rapist. One manslaughter freak and a child abuser on a perjury rap.

JAMES: Hale-fuckin'-luhja! Some wise guys, huh?

RACHEL: We're smarter than they are.

JAMES: Correction. Rachel Bloom's smarter. I gotta present for you. For you! (*He gives her a ring.*)

RACHEL: A ring! You're so corny!

JAMES: Won it in a crap game.

RACHEL: A crap game? This, I love!

JAMES: The dice weren't loaded. Keep it – a token of my appreciation. First step on the road to Downtown Paradise.

RACHEL (*amused*): You're full of shit!

JAMES (*smooching, laughing. Whispers*): What's it to be? The bed or the wall?

RACHEL (*playing coy*): Mmmh? The wall was sorta nice. Never had the wall with Nathan. What say we test the bedsprings?

JAMES: Ever seen fingertip press-ups from below? Never do less than a hundred.

RACHEL: You're all talk!

JAMES: We got ninety seconds!

They rush to the bed.

Blackout.

Scene Two – 'Way Out!'

Prison cell, San Felipe, Califonia, August 1970.

JAMES: They killed Oscar. Wise up! The Santanero prison authorities are culpable.

RACHEL: It was a fight over drugs money. The killer confessed. He had a knife wound.

JAMES: That don' prove nothin'.

RACHEL: Oscar's prints on the handle. Both had coke in their blood samples.

JAMES: It was set up, damn you!

RACHEL: That'll take a whole heap of proving in court.

JAMES: In court? You kiddin'? You crazy? I'm next! Johnny Silver, Lou Stevens, now Oscar. How much genocide do you need? I'll never get out of here alive! Never!

RACHEL (*appealing*): We have a trial date.

JAMES: Ain't gonna be no trial. I sure as hell ain't stickin' around for no posthumous 'Not Guilty' verdict. There's got to be another way.

RACHEL: My way's the only way. Right now I'm concerned that Watts' drug involvement doesn't rub off on you.

JAMES: Don't try to sanitize me!

RACHEL: What's eating you? There's something else. I know it.

JAMES: You've read 'Black Horizons'?

RACHEL: Read it? I got Herbie the goddam publisher!

JAMES: 'Comrade' Hamilton. Oh yeah. Skipped to Cuba, 'to build the army of black liberation'. Then early retirement with all the Cuban pussy he can hump.

RACHEL: It was a great book!

JAMES: Thought you'd say that.

RACHEL: What's up? Did I fail my grades or something?

JAMES: No clarity of purpose, Counsellor. No programme. (*Picks up book.*) My book was set to change all that.

163

RACHEL: Can we cut the coded messages and get to the point?

JAMES (*slamming book down*): What happened to my last chapter?

RACHEL: 'Final Reckonings'? There was a word limit.

JAMES: So you cut my programme – without which none of it amounts to a hill of beans. When you cut that chapter you put me in the same ball-park as Hamilton.

RACHEL: It would have damaged your case and split the defence committee.

JAMES: So! You did censor me!

RACHEL: 'Censor'? Have you any idea what the use of phrases like 'the final solution' would have on white liberal opinion?

JAMES: I don't give a fuck about white liberal opinion.

RACHEL: Hitler used that phrase!

JAMES: Stop trying to conduct the orchestra! Hamilton and Redmond have sold out.

RACHEL: They're not even on speaking terms anymore! Fighting each other for control.

JAMES: And I am fighting both of them. Hamilton knows it. When he made me Brigadier General, it was his last throw to buy me off.

RACHEL: Excuse me. I'm really not into male competitive games. Haven't we got enough enemies, enough problems?

JAMES: It's about leadership.

RACHEL: It's a dance of death! I spent the whole past year getting Herbie Hamilton out of jail. Then he turns on Redmond and you turn on both of them! For Christ's sake – communicate.

JAMES: Impossible with people you fundamentally disagree with. Have you read Mao on 'Liberated Zones'? – also cut from my book.

RACHEL: This is America, not goddam Imperial China!

JAMES: You're already behind events. The pace is hotting up.

RACHEL: Don't give me that 'revolution' stuff again. I've left playschool.

JAMES: We need an army. We already have groups training in the mountains.

RACHEL: Yes, and bodies. Unexplained killings.

JAMES: What would you do with informers?

RACHEL: How do you know they were informers?

JAMES (*touches his nose*): Confidential. I have lines of communication.

RACHEL: What do you want? To fight the Civil War over?

JAMES: That's what young blacks want.

RACHEL: Guerilla warfare? You wouldn't have a hope in hell!

JAMES (*sits*): When I want a military adviser I'll ask for one.

RACHEL (*kneeling by his knee*): James, please. Don't go down this path. It will destroy you, the movement, everything. In a few months time, you'll have a new life.

JAMES (*stands as she remains kneeling. He ridicules and parodies a Luther King speech*): 'I have a dream. That one day on the red hills of Georgia, the sons of former slave owners will be able to sit down together at the table of brotherhood. I have a dream that...'

RACHEL (*cuts in on the cruel parody to restore its dignity*): 'My four little children will one day live in a nation, where they will not be judged by the colour of their skin, but by the content of their characters. I have a dream...'

Short silence.

JAMES: If Earl Ray hadn't shot him, we'd've had to.

RACHEL: Where's your humanity, James? They took it from you?

JAMES: You, a white woman, ask me that?

RACHEL: James, I'm scared.

JAMES: You look it too!

RACHEL: Not for myself. I'm scared for you! I'm scared that at your moment of triumph, you'll throw it all away in some futile gesture of defiance.

JAMES: I ain't in no longevity contest. When you're dead, people respect you. If you're black, s'about the only time they do.

RACHEL: Please... James.

JAMES: The only way to stop yourself bein' pushed around is to become a warrior. The Jews learned that in Israel.

RACHEL: I'm not a Zionist!

JAMES: Then you should be! Jews have their own land now. That's where I'd be if I was a Jew.

RACHEL: America is my home.

JAMES: Till they come for you with flaming torches, cattle trucks. Give 'em time!

RACHEL: It was America defeated Hitler.

JAMES: The Red Army defeated Hitler. We have to rediscover who we are.

RACHEL: You're as American as the rest of us.

JAMES: Afro-Americans – one time a race of warriors! A warrior is a superior person. A whole generation has to relearn that. Then we stop breeding slaves. We become men.

RACHEL (*stands up*): Great! So, you lose one half your support. What kind of woman cares for a child for eighteen years so he can die in battle?

JAMES: My kind of woman.

RACHEL: And those who don't?

JAMES: They must hide away in the shadows. Keep their chastity. Do you know the great thing about violence?

RACHEL: Can't think of one right now.

JAMES: If you don't care about your own life, if it's subordinate to some historical destiny, then you have power over those afraid of death.

RACHEL: Forgive me, but I've had it up to here with terror tactics. It's just nihilism.

JAMES: So? I'm a nihilist.

RACHEL: You believe in nothing?

JAMES: I'm a wild nigger. And I seek a vengeance that is cosmic! You say I'll destroy myself, but they're destroying us. Forced to live in shanty towns below the white temples of their paradise. I'm gonna pull it all down!

RACHEL: Samson, huh? Pulling down the temples?

JAMES: How much is in the Defence fund?

RACHEL (*sighs angrily*): There are some authorisations you need to sign.

JAMES: Leaving how much?

RACHEL: Nine hundred and thirty thousand.

JAMES: What you doin'? Accumulatin' interest on government bonds?

RACHEL: We don't keep sums like that in the bathroom cabinet!

JAMES: Can't help yourself, can you. Everything you touch turns to gold. Even a dirty nigger with a prison record.

RACHEL: Am I getting your drift? What do you...

JAMES: You said I had authorisation.

RACHEL: I deeply resent your insinuations! I deserve better than this. I who have made this campaign my whole life! You insult me!

JAMES (*puts a piece of paper and a pen down in front of her*): Say that you, on instructions of your client...

RACHEL: 'Client?' It's come to that! (*She writes hurriedly.*)

JAMES: Hereby authorise the transfer of the entire Defence committee funds...

RACHEL: Some of it rightly belongs to Watts.

JAMES: Send something to his mother – ten thousand? The remainder to be transferred to the account of the Black Liberation Front.

RACHEL (*as she signs*): You realise that my signing this incriminates me. It's a paramilitary organisation – against the constitution.

JAMES: I'm sure President Nixon will understand. He knows all about that.

RACHEL: Thanks a bunch. The FBI now have all they need to indict me.

JAMES: You know perfectly well they'd never do that.

RACHEL (*throws down pen, angrily*): What did you say?

JAMES: Now hear this. I run this outfit. Where you comin' from? Where'd you learn to be such an operator?

RACHEL (*crying, angrily*): I am deeply hurt by your remarks and I'm mourning for the James Wilson I once knew.

JAMES: Thought you knew! I want that money transferred to train an army. (*Whispers loudly.*) I'm bustin' outa here. We need guns. We need a helicopter.

RACHEL (*distraught and shaking*): Don't tell me anymore. I will not collude in your suicide.

JAMES (*hands her the paper*): Just do it!

RACHEL: Can I go now please. I'm all through here. Needless to say, once these funds are transferred, you will cease to be my client. I can recommend someone if you'd like.

JAMES: Think you can jus' walk out on me?

RACHEL: I'm not quitting. You are!

Rachel steps forward. Bars descend as she dries her eyes.

JAMES (*kindly*): Rachel. I never was what you tried to make me. I'm from the downtown streets – ain't made for paradise. You would never allow yourself to know me as I am. Whatever happens, it's not your fault. None of it was.

Footsteps. Sound of keys.

Quick Fade.

Scene Three – False Dawn

A penthouse, Hong Kong, 1982. RACHEL enters stage left, in front of curtain/darkened stage, in wheelchair as in Prologue.

RACHEL: That was the last time I ever saw James Wilson. He died, with his comrades, in the attempted break-out. Three prison guards had their throats cut. It was a vision of hell. I turned my back on the movement. Old friends on the left would cross the street when they saw me coming. I was branded as 'a traitor' and, get this, 'an agent of the FBI'! But gradually, over the years, I found the strength to know myself. I moved east, to New York and here I came to realise that that noble aspiration of our constitution 'the pursuit of happiness', was not a crime, that I had a right to be happy. And then something wonderful happened. It was like a warm wind in winter. I simply fell in love with another woman. As you can imagine, it didn't go down too well with my mother! But, Meryl and I moved in together with my two kids and we set up a practice in women's law. No more defending killers, just deserving cases. We were... so happy! It seemed like I'd finally atoned for my past. That was my second big mistake – for the sins of our youth shall be visited upon us when we least expect it. It was almost ten years later and I'd just got home from work.

A telephone begins to ring. RACHEL wheels herself off, stage left.

Fade.

Scene Four – Pay Off

A smart New York apartment, 1980. RACHEL is fully fit in this scene. She enters and picks up the telephone.

RACHEL: Yvonne? Hi honey! How was the conference? Good. Good. Oh you're back! Here, in New York?

The doorbell rings.

Oh. I've got a caller. Will I pick you up or will you grab a cab? OK. Gotta go. Love you too. Bye! (*She quickly goes to the door. The intruder is on the doorstep dressed in a balaclava or mask.*)

INTRUDER (*pushes her inside*): You Rachel Bloom?

RACHEL: Hey, easy, huh! I am, yes.

INTRUDER: Over there, in the chair. Fast!

RACHEL: Do I know you? What do you want?

INTRUDER walks to telephone, disconnects it. Pulls curtains.

RACHEL: If it's money, that's not a problem. (*Picks up her handbag from the couch.*)

INTRUDER (*rips bag from her hands, rummages through it*): Don't get smart. How much is in here?

RACHEL: Sixty, seventy dollars. I'm not sure.

INTRUDER: Credit cards?

RACHEL: In the bag.

INTRUDER (*stuffs bag into leather jacket*): Got any jewelry?

RACHEL: Don't wear jewelry anymore.

INTRUDER: Don't a dyke pretty herself up for another dyke?

RACHEL (*stands*): Hey mister!

INTRUDER (*pushes her back into chair, violently*): She a white dyke or black dyke?

RACHEL: How d'you know about me?

171

INTRUDER: Call me, your confessor. Bitch, you are notorious. You are a fuckin' legend.

RACHEL I'm not intimidated by the likes of you.

INTRUDER (*chuckles*): You prejudiced against black folks?

RACHEL: You've got me all wrong, buster.

INTRUDER: Then why you sleepin' with a white woman?

RACHEL: She's my partner.

INTRUDER: How d'you get it up her, huh? What d'you use?

RACHEL (*stands. walks to door*): Get out! Get outa here!

INTRUDER pulls gun from belt.

RACHEL: Oh my God!

INTRUDER: You not gittin' the picture, are you? (*Pushes her back in chair. Thinks he hears noise upstairs.*) What's that? (*Strides around, looking at ceiling.*)

RACHEL: Nobody. The place is empty. But my partner'll be back any minute.

INTRUDER: Nice one. But I happen to know she's at a conference in Berkeley. What you think I am – a hustler, petty thief?

RACHEL: You could have fooled me.

INTRUDER: I live the way I have to live, because I'm forced to live this way, honkey.

RACHEL (*folds arms*): Tell that to a social worker! You are what you are because you chose to be that way, buster! I've been defending black people, black men mostly, all of my professional life.

INTRUDER: Reg'lar li'l Luther King, ain't ya?

RACHEL: You're not fit to mention his name.

INTRUDER: Wow! Passion! I'll bet you're real good between the sheets!

RACHEL (*stands*): Is it a fuck you want? OK, whip out your whang and let's get it over with. Ev'ry man's dream, to screw a lesbian. It's your lucky day.

INTRUDER: I don' need no charity, lady. I'm beautiful!

RACHEL: Prove it! Take your mask off!

INTRUDER: Heh heh heh! Devious, cunning Delilah! No way you goin' a see mah face.

RACHEL: You're scared?

INTRUDER: No. But you should be.

RACHEL: We're a brave people. We've seen off thousands of shit-heads like you – strutting arrogant little male bastards. We've survived.

INTRUDER: James Wilson didn't.

RACHEL is silent, anxious.

INTRUDER: Kinda quiet suddenly?

RACHEL (*bites lip, drops her head*): I'll never forget him.

INTRUDER: Sure you won't. Shot to pieces by a tower guard. Mus' be nine years now.

RACHEL: I had nothing to do with that.

INTRUDER: You were his attorney.

RACHEL: Not by then I wasn't.

INTRUDER: You knew the break-out plan. Then you quit his case. Now why'd you do that?

RACHEL: Because I loved him.

INTRUDER: You ditched 'im.

RACHEL: I didn't. He walked out on me. I could have saved him. Got him free. After Herbie Hamilton's release we were all set.

INTRUDER: Herbie Hamilton – another quitter. Lives in a f-i-i-i-ne house. Why he's a chat show celebrity now. You made him that. You turned Hamilton from a panther into an aristo-cat, lickin' the cream and writin' his memoirs. I don't think you ever believed in none of it.

RACHEL (*stands in tears but defiant*): I still do, God help me! I still do. I begged James but he wouldn't listen. And we were that close. I wanted him out so we could be together.

INTRUDER: James Wilson had your number baby!

RACHEL: Don't call me 'baby'!

INTRUDER: Oh, he was all wised up about you. You think you were the only white cheer-leader he screwed in his cell? Why, they were queuein' up for him, all those fancy white prison visitors...

RACHEL: Spare me this!

INTRUDER: He used to bribe the pigs with coke-money to keep look-out.

RACHEL: Don't say that!

INTRUDER: And you loved it.

RACHEL: Don't, please don't.

INTRUDER: Because it's true I know.

RACHEL: James was everything I ever aspired to in those times. When he died, movement seemed to fall apart.

INTRUDER: This won't save you.

RACHEL: Who are you?

INTRUDER: Call me an avenging angel. Keep talkin'. There are things I need to know.

RACHEL: Were you in gaol with James Wilson?

INTRUDER: Don't get personal.

RACHEL: You're in the movement?

INTRUDER: We talkin' 'bout you, not me.

RACHEL: There isn't any more to say.

INTRUDER: Think of somethin'. You don' have a lot of time.

RACHEL: What do you mean?

INTRUDER: So you in the property law now, jes' like your Momma always wanted for you?

RACHEL: You did know James?

INTRUDER: Down to business. So you turned your back on us. You turned your back on men, too. When did you turn your back on the FBI?

RACHEL: What are you talking about?

INTRUDER (*checks the window*): All adds up.

RACHEL: They still check on me. I'm involved in lawsuits on black welfare – voluntary – no payment!

INTRUDER: Good for you, Saint Rachel. Don't get me wrong. I'm not sayin you work for the Feds exclusively.

RACHEL (*angrily*): I have never worked for them!

INTRUDER: Wilson thought so. Tol' me so. Right now the movement has some – splits.

RACHEL: Tell me about it! What's new! I'm sick of all that cannibalism!

INTRUDER loads revolver instantly. Startles RACHEL.

INTRUDER: You call me a cannibal? (*Puts gun to her head.*)

RACHEL: No... no... no... that's not what I meant. Please put the gun away.

INTRUDER: Get a pen, paper! Write!

RACHEL (*fetches them, sensing a reprieve*): Write what?

INTRUDER (*training the gun on her*): I, Rachel Bloom...

RACHEL (*writes, shaking with fear*): I, Rachel Bloom... sorry, my hands are shaking...

INTRUDER: Hereby confess that I...

RACHEL: Hereby confess that I... this is not my best handwriting... confess what?

INTRUDER: That I did conspire with federal agencies to fix up James Wilson in the prison shoot-out...

RACHEL (*firmly, stands up unafraid*): Oh no. Oh no! That is not true!

INTRUDER: Write it, bitch.

RACHEL: I will not write lies!

The doorbell rings. There is a tense pause. Both of them are thinking fast. He glances towards the door, alarmed. She too is alarmed for her partner's safety. She advances on him. He backs towards the door. She rushes past him to bar his way to the door. She opens the door and yells.

RACHEL: Run, Yvonne, run! Call the police! Run baby!

The INTRUDER backs in again towards the centre of the room, his gun is still nervously trained on RACHEL. RACHEL stands in doorframe, arms outstretched, holding the doorposts to prevent him passing and to protect her partner.

INTRUDER: Out of the way! Move, or you're a dead woman!

RACHEL stands defiantly, breathing heavily with fear. Slowly he takes aim. RACHEL backs out through the door, leaving the door open. The INTRUDER advances to the door and takes aim again, shooting four deliberate shots in the sign of the cross. We hear RACHEL shriek, followed by groans. He tucks the gun in his belt, glances around the room, grabs her signed 'confession' and strides out.

Fade to near darkness.

To prevent a false ending, we hear voices off, whilst RACHEL is preparing a wheelchair entrance for the last scene.

VOICE: Oh my God! Get an ambulance somebody! Hurry!

VOICE: She's still breathing!

VOICE: Rachel! Rachel! Can you hear me honey? Hold on there honey! Hold on! Jesus! She's shot real bad!

VOICE: They're on their way!

VOICE: Don't move her! Don't move her!

VOICE: Get a blanket, a coat or something. Rachel! They're here now. You're going to be all right, do you hear me. You're gonna be just fine!

We hear the approach of ambulance sirens. Flashing red lights illuminate front of stage. A few seconds pass. Then Rachel slowly appears stage left, in a wheelchair.

Lights come up again.

Scene Five – Epilogue

A penthouse, Hong Kong, 1982.

RACHEL: So they rushed me to emergency and opened me up. The surgeons said the bullet wounds formed the pattern of a crucifix. Ain't that weird? I think about that a lot. They didn't think I'd make it through, but I wanted to live. Even though I'll never walk again and I'm incontinent. I wanted to nail that bastard! We were all under twenty-four / seven police protection, the whole family. I told Meryl it was over between us. She cried, but I insisted – for her sake, not mine. I still miss her terribly. Not a day goes by I don't think about her and what we had together. And now, for the first time in my life I was on the side of the police and the forces of law and order. I learned to shoot a revolver for my own protection. Here it is! (*Holds up revolver.*) I keep it on me every hour of the day. My assailant's name was Lincoln Winter. He went down for life and I was chief prosecution witness. Winter had been an accomplice of James Wilson. He led a group called the 'Black Guerrilla Family', a euphemism for drug racketeering and extortion. My former comrades on the left still see them as, what's the word, 'revolutionaries!' Tell me about it! There was a time I wanted to change the world, top to bottom. Oh yeah! Start history over on a clean page. Now I just wish things could be the way they were when I was a whole person, with legs that worked and someone to just love! And now, well here I am, in exile in a secure penthouse suite in old Hong Kong. In fear of my life. Life! This is 'life'? Do I want to live at all? (*She addresses the revolver.*) What do you think my

178

friend, do you call this living? (*To audience.*) He says the jury's out on that one. Perhaps I'll be lucky. Perhaps this time the verdict will go against me. I hope so. Because you know, and this is the worst of it, even though I tried to do right all my life as a radical, I was part of a destructive generation. My road to hell was paved with noble aspirations. And in my heart I still feel, guilty! Yes, oh my God, I feel... guilty!

The lights fade to utter darkness. A shot rings out. The opening bars of Elgar's cello concerto end on a sombre and sonorous low note.

The End.

MR OWEN'S MILLENNIUM

Original Cast

Robert Owen   -   Owen Garmon

Director   -   Steve Fisher

Scene One – The Blithe Country

The setting is the same for all scenes. The Bear Hotel, Newtown, Montgomeryshire, 1858 – the year of Owen's death. Owen in long nightshirt and blanket, sits centre-stage in a chair designed by Howell Harris, which is throne-like. The chair has winding steps to a pulpit, above. Blackout. Slow fade up to floor spot.

Who's there? A silhouette against the dying light? Speak!

No-one. No-one.

And yet....

Twilight is deceptive. One half-sees half-things in this grey time between day and night. Between life....

Mrs Williams! The fire. More coal, Mrs Williams!

I like it here – The Bear Hotel – finest inn in Newtown. I feel at home. I am at home, near enough....

I was born there, on the other side of that wall. Eighty-seven years ago. There in the postmaster's shop, my father's house.

Strange to be back, seventy years at least since last I was in Newtown. Mrs Williams! It will go out! Mrs Williams! (*To audience.*) If you want anything done in life, do it yourself.

Mrs Williams thinks I ought to see a priest. Not today thank you. No priest. Superstitious nonsense! Gave that up when I was ten.

Pause.

I've got my own religion, up here. (*Taps his forehead.*) Rational religion. Worked it out myself. I know exactly where the church goes wrong. I tell them often enough. 'Rational thought will triumph over blind faith!' They don't like it. Don't like that at all.

In Bristol, they overturn my carriage! I have to be rescued from a screaming mob sent wild by rabble-rousing clergymen and acting in a most un-Christian manner. I proclaim, 'Follow me. I am the way, the truth and the light!' Not a wise move. 'Blasphemer! Heretic! Antichrist!'

Well, I've outlived my adversaries. Long dead most of them. I speak to their spirits and they all admit now that I was right. But at the time, at the time... do you think they'd listen to the voice of reason?

It's been hard, I tell you.

There were occasions I thought I was going mad. To know the answers to the problems of society, and not to be believed. For let me tell you this – I did know! It could have worked. It did work. It will work.

Ah, If only the characters of men were better formed, they could see the logic of it, make my system flesh!

The problem is, first, to create a society to make men's character more rational.

He stands, drops blanket, goes to trousers. Changes mind.

The Duke of Wellington, long-dead now, said to me only the other day, 'Dear Mr Owen' he said, 'your plan for community villages should have been adopted by the Government.' That would have abolished unemployment for all time!

Pause.

Yet, he never did embrace the plan when he was alive, when he was Prime Minister. They all admit that I am right, all the spirits. Wisdom after the event, see.

Community villages, that's my answer. My answer to this irrational system of man against man. Man against woman. Greed and Profit! Villages of harmony, peace, co-operation, all over the land. The world!

He walks to a small model village which glows, white.

Here, houses for working people with bedrooms for the children. Factories, owned by these same folk. Schools! Halls for music, dancing and discussions on the management of affairs, philosophy.

I had thought one time of making model folk. To people it. But model folk are hard to make. Many will not stand on their own two feet, keep falling over. So! I dispensed with them. Well, you get the idea. That's the important thing – the idea!

He puts on trousers.

You know some... call me 'dreamer'. Dreamer! I am the Dreamer who cuts the working day, and makes it pay!

Aye. There's the trick. To make it pay! I am rich, rich beyond my wildest expectations before the age of twenty-three. Dreams indeed! I live them. And I start with... nothing. Not a penny. Right here. In Newtown.

Lights dim to near black for a moment. Lights up.

My father is both postmaster and saddlemaker. My mother, a Williams of Vaynor. Farmers, from these hills where Welsh is spoken. I am a happy child in this blithe country. From here you can see Newtown Hall, the squire's residence. Old Sir John, a kind man, but, very strange.

I'm told that in his upstairs room, lit by a single flickering candle, he is wont to sit bolt upright in his bed. Either side of him his two dead wives, embalmed and white. He... loves them, you see. Or rather, he continues to love them after they die. If you take my meaning.

So now, his third wife refuses to share his bed until the corpses are removed. A not unreasonable request. In England, his behaviour might be thought odd, but here in Wales....

He pulls up socks.

Circumstances fashion us to what we are become. 'The character of man is made for him and not by him.' This has always been my firm belief. I never thought man 'inherently evil', lazy or dishonest. We are all fashioned by circumstance, but change the circumstance and you can change the man.

He picks up shoes, holds them.

My circumstances must have been fortunate despite my lowly origins. At school, the master – a Mr Thicknesse (Yes, Thicknesse – there's a name) is stern at times, though not with me. For I'm abnormal in my lust for books and he struggles to keep up with me. By the age of seven I am teaching my fellows. It's the making of me. I set about the task with earnestness. I learn by helping others learn! The power of collective enlightenment!

Some men, like the Squire, are born with privilege, but learning is the greatest privilege of all. The path ahead no longer lies in darkness and I, I can lead the way. But it's a long path. And it leads me, far away from here.

He puts on shoes.

Newtown is woven out of wool. Everywhere, small weavers cottages, and above them all, a single common workshop for the looms. Wool comes to live next door to me when three maiden sisters – Misses... Tilsley – open a draper's shop which wraps itself around me like a shawl.

I'd fallen from a horse. And the eldest of these ladies calls to ask about my health. 'Drapery' says she, 'is not given to physical hazards.'

She shows me to how to buy a roll of cloth, cut it into lengths and sell at twice the price. So simple! She is a Methodist, this Miss Tilsley. And I am most impressed with her methods.

I'm now a proper little merchant, and give thanks to God for wearing cotton robes as he patrols the skies.

My dear parents never tell me what I should believe and so I read books on all aspects of philosophy, borrowed from the libraries of local clergymen.

Only once, as a child, am I ever punished. For what I can't recall! Some good reason. My father beats me with a whip to gain compliance, but I do not yield.

I am convinced that punishment is useless. Worse, injurious to the punisher. My father was tortured with remorse at his own actions; my only suffering was for him. I soon forgot, but he could not forgive himself.

Oh! When we abuse what we most love. To beat a child... we kill the best part of ourselves and pass on to innocents the stains of this immoral world.

It's cold in here. Even here in the womb of my universe. As cold as on that day I took the coach from Shrewsbury to London and said goodbye for ever to my home. 'Goodbye, Dada! Da boch chi Mam!' I was only ten, but the time had come for me to seek my fortune in the world. In my pocket, one silver shilling. In my heart, a lump like lead.

Fade.

Scene Two – The Romance of Business

Lights up to general wash.

By sixteen I'm a veteran of the retail trade, having had a long affair with drapery.

He holds the blanket.

Flannelette, fustian, hessian, wool! Silk, satin, organdie and lace. I know the feel of it, the smell of it, the price-at-which-you-sell of it!

He puts on waistcoat.

At nineteen I have arrived! I am a cotton merchant. Apple dumplings every day and money in the bank. Life is fine, so when the owner of the largest, newest cotton-spinning factory on the planet is looking for a manager I knock on the door and state my terms. 'Three hundred a year and, oh, my name on all the labels!'

He faints, recovers, he offers me the job. Fame at last! 'Owen' is on every gentleman's lips and all the ladies camisoles!

Ah! The Romance of Business. And the Business of Romance. I confess that I am hopeless with women. Awkward, blushing, stammering. Lowering my eyes as if I were the maid.

So, when introduced to Miss Caroline Dale, whose father happens to be the founder of the Bank of Scotland, all my practical gallantry and repartee is summoned up. Shuffling my feet, looking everywhere but at the lady, mumbling incoherently like a stable lad, reverting to the Welsh peasant, even in prosperity.

This vulnerability of mine she finds... irresistible! A mutual friend reminds me it was Caroline who had arranged for me to tour her father's mill at Lanark. 'Did-I-not-see-a-meaning-in-that?'

This lady of such fair countenance and charm wants none but me for a husband! And she the eldest with no brothers! This is a language I understand. No chasing, hide-and-seek. No clandestine meeting, fumbling in the dark. A businesslike romance.

The third time I meet her, it is love at first sight! But, her father is religious. Devout even! The founder, the founder, no less, of an independent Scottish church with an intense dislike of Englishmen. So I speak a few choice words to him in Welsh. 'Bore da, Syr. Shwd ych chi? Hoffwn y fraint o briodi eich merch, Caroline.' He does not understand. But it seems to do the trick, especially when I offer to pay sixty thousand for a share in his Lanark mill.

It may not sound very romantic, but that was how the love of my life began! And she loved me! We were... productive. Four boys, three girls, survive to bind us ever more fondly to each other.

He holds up a 'silent monitor'; a cube.

When we start, there are bad lads in the mill village. Drinking?! They would go on a 'spree' that lasted days. Too blind drunk to work. They beat their wives, fight in the streets, and rouse the diligent from their sleep. Look at this! That's what they get. (*He turns the cube to show its black side.*) A black square, hung above their position in the workshop. But when their conduct and performance improve...

He turns the cube to show its blue side.

I pay them steady wages. Never lay them off when business is slack. This is appreciated. Pretty soon...

He turns the cube to show its yellow side.

Yellow squares begin to appear at most positions in the factory. Drunkenness declines and so does wife-beating.

Fresh food in the shop. Those who want their whisky have to walk for it. They begin to believe in themselves, acquire dignity. The results are remarkable.

With a flourish, he turns the cube to show its white side.

Excellent! You see? My own invention. The silent monitor. No punishment. Improvement of conditions! And profits rise! Yes, profits rise!

I stop the children working, straightaway! To school, they go. Music, dancing, drawing, all day! Reading, writing for the older ones. I pay the teachers from my own pocket, because it works!

My system works. But my business partners are not satisfied, always looking over my shoulder, looking to increase their profits.

I ask them, 'What man needs more than five per cent return?' They answer, 'He whose competitors make ten and steal the march on him.' 'Right' I say, 'That's it!' I ditch them. Buy them out. 'Goodbye! No hard feelings! Take your capital elsewhere!' And they call themselves Christians!

My denigrators disguise their greed with sly remarks. By this time, it matters not a fig what they say. Politicians, men of business, bishops, princes and philosophers are lining up to see Mr Owen's great experiment!

My name is whispered on the lips of destiny. Nothing bars my progress to the highest offices, the marble halls of power, to counsel kings and fashion fate. Yet all I've achieved is but the preface to a deeper purpose.

One night, as I lie asleep, Reason, in robes of whitest cotton, pokes me in the ribs and breathes aloud, 'Robert, you dine with giants at their feast. But if the loaf's... a mountain, wherein lies the yeast?

'Robert, is it mere sorcery that makes the beanstalk grow? A man of science really ought to know.'

'Robert, if you seek the source of wealth and value, look in your heart.'

And then I knew what I must do. Remake the world anew. That's all! Remake the world anew!

Fade.

Scene Three – A Light in the Darkness

Snap to flood lighting.

The seat of power lies in Parliament. To Westminster and fight the battle there. Caroline pleads with me, 'Teach them by example. Your power lies here.' Her gentle wisdom cannot quell my angry conscience.

Influential friends in London praise my book, 'A New View of Society'. Sir Robert Peel promises to lay my reforms before the House. But first, they set up a committee! And this committee sits, and sits, and sits. 'To examine whether Mr Owen's proposal represents interference with the management of private business.'

Of course it does! That is its purpose! I demand that the Government 'remit the tax upon raw cotton imports... and prevent the employment of children under twelve years old in cotton or other mills; and limit the hours of work to twelve per day....'

And now a sub-committee, if you please, to investigate my 'allegation' that fifteen hours work a day is indeed damaging to children's health! Committees, committees, committees! And all around them, an inferno of despair! Soldiers, returning from the wars in France discard their badges and insignia. Napoleon is banished. No need of men to fight him. No need of cloth for uniforms. No need of labour to make cloth.

They're still discussing factory reform while all around them the factories are shutting down. And on top of this, the price of bread keeps rising.

'I am persuaded of the absolute necessity of repealing the Corn Laws which keep the landlords fat by preventing import of cheap grain to feed the people!'

I do not, will not, ever understand the immorality that puts profit before living souls. The very fabric of society frays like rotted sack-cloth.

What tapestry is woven now? Its weft – the price of corn. Its warp – starvation. Its texture – sharp as bayonet points. Its colour – red as blood!

I warn, but the authorities are deaf. They throw out my plan and slam the door on reason!

He mounts the rostrum. Sounds of thunder, lightning.

'The time is at hand for the fulfilment of all things. For in the last days of misery there shall be signs in the sun and in the moon... and in the stars... and, upon the earth, distress of nations with perplexity... and men's hearts failing for fear of those things which are coming – for the power of heaven shall be broken!'

I am called 'Prophet', yet I only give voice to the thunder. I am called 'Visionary', yet I only see what the lightning makes visible, the tortured forms of men....

The storm rages but the primitives who rule us disregard the lightning and its crashing echoes; disregard the elemental force of history! They turn their anger upon me! I am spurned by the establishment. So, I spurn them! I take my message to the people. I call a meeting at The City of London Tavern.

'A country can never be beneficially wealthy while it supports a large proportion of its working classes in idle poverty and useless occupation... ignorance and poverty demoralises the inhabitants and makes them vicious... so that strong coercion and cruel punishment must necessarily follow... that discontent and opposition to those who govern must inevitably ensue... that while these incentives to everything vile and criminal shall be permitted and encouraged by the Government, it is downright mockery to talk about improving the morals of the working classes!'

'How does this rotten system work? Simple! Every day they take – everything the people make! By contrast, my Villages of Unity and Co-operation will give the people control of the circumstances which govern their lives... the common ownership of their place of work and all the wealth that they create. Gentlemen, I am not your religion, nor any yet propounded in this world! Don't look to God for help! It's time to put away childish things! Yes! Man can make himself!'

A voice in the crowd shouts, 'Socialist!'

I've never heard the word before and nor has any man. Something new is brought into the world, this day. Some novel creed to fire the aspirations of an age of turbulence! My creed, which men shall wrestle with, as once they wrestled with God.

They call me 'Messiah without faith' because my faith lies in man and woman. I know this infant scheme of things, half-formed and grossly premature yet squawking lustily, is of my body and my blood... I am the father; this is my son!

Thunder.

Fade.

Scene Four – Adventures in Paradise

Lights up to general wash, exuding hope and optimism. Owen steps downstage.

England is all wrong. Each man in his allotted place! Here, the king; there, the nobleman; the squire – here! Now, the businessman! What to do with him? Oh! Over there somewhere. And what have we here? The common people! Tread them underfoot!

Reform? We'll have no more of that!

The future has been postponed indefinitely. 'Pick up your shovels. Touch your forelocks. Pray to God on Sundays. Carry on... existing.'

That's why I never joined the clamour for the right to vote. What use is Parliament when men don't own the means by which they live?!

But, America. America! Where dreams are lived. Exodus and Revelations, all in one. America! A place to grow! Each horizon brings a never-ending paradise.

A Mr Flower arrives in New Lanark from America to sell me the Garden of Eden, so I buy it, cheap at twice the price. (I knock him down a bit of course. Supply is plentiful, demand is slack.) A town in Indiana called 'Harmony'. Just my kind of place.

Streets planted with black locust trees and mulberry. Vineyards, orchards, dwelling houses, community halls, factories, pasture and magnificent cornfields. I pack my bags and take my sons along with me. We sail for America!

He runs to the pulpit stairs and mounts the rostrum.

I announce a new Empire of Peace and Goodwill to men. I present President Quincy Adams with a model of our planned community and invite the industrious and well-disposed of all nations to join us at... New Harmony!

To great rejoicing a small group of us sail off down the Ohio River. We're a mixed bunch. Philosophers; writers; experts in zoology and botany; pedagogues; doctors; two bankers; one engineer; and a specialist in astronomy – indispensable for such a venture. A boatload of knowledge!

Occasionally some native Indians appear upon the distant banks. We greet them and raise our hats to show our benevolent intentions. They do not return our felicitations, but simply stare.

In New Harmony, people of many nations flock to us. Every type is represented – skilled artisans and labourers; the literate and untutored. My son, William, warns me that our recruits are not entirely without blemish. Some are perfect drones, others lazy theorists, and there is a fair smattering of unprincipled sharpers.

We are mostly men, so women are in short supply at dancing in the evening. So much so that we introduce a ballot to allocate female partners to the ugly men. Not a few of these young maids dash off in floods of tears, complaining that freedom of choice is essential in matters so personal.

The Indians are... still watching us, rivetted by our behaviour no doubt. We think it best to organise... artillery, just as a precaution. The Indians move farther off, but still they watch.

He descends from the rostrum.

In a short span of four months I am sufficiently encouraged by our progress to announce the 'New State of Existence'. All things held in common. No money; credit notes are given for work done. Complete equality between the sexes; the family abolished; a society open to all – except, of course, the negro slaves.

There is dancing in the streets.

One day a genteel woman of the German aristocracy (we attract all sorts), comes to see me to complain of... milking duties. Could she not wear gloves for this distasteful operation?

I do not object, but the cows do. So we put her with the pigs. She claims the porkers do not show her due respect. So we put her in with the sheep. She gets thoroughly bored as a shepherdess. In the end we put her with the horses. This is just what she was looking for. She rides off on one of them. We never saw her again.

The Germans never really hit it off with the English. This emerges very early on. The French look down on everybody. I notice, in the evenings, the intellectuals choose to gather at one end of our Hall of Communal Brotherhood. The artisans gather at the other, complaining bitterly of 'theorisers', who avoid hard graft. I have some sympathy with this observation, till one of them indicts me and some distinguished guests for drinking all the tea! Still, to show my confidence and my good faith, I relinquish all my private holdings, making it a true collective. All is going excellently!

The children's welfare remains of great importance to me. They hardly ever see their parents, so that the stains of older generations shall not be nourished in them. There is no punishment, and no scourge for idleness.

The effect on them is quite remarkable! Thoroughly rebellious, even barbarous. I see in some of them that... look, I had observed on the faces of the Indians as they watched us from the river bank.

We decide it's best to return to the family structure. For the time being. Those parents who have dispensed with marriage cause great offence to the religious folk amongst us, and they suggest two separate communities. Soon we have three, five, ten communities. Four years of this leaves me exhausted and my fortune spent.

The characters of men, too firmly fashioned by a heartless world, are ill-suited to the mammoth task I set them.

I can't pretend I'm not dispirited on the voyage back to England. I shun the other passengers, turn inwards on myself. Three score years, now home to Caroline and to my daughters. Peace and quiet.

On the coach to Scotland, a gentleman reading The Times recognises me. 'Look at this', he says. It speaks of unions, forming everywhere, co-operatives and the free exchange of goods. A mighty movement. They call it 'Owenism'! And The Times doesn't like it!

Quick fade to darkness.

Scene Five – Redeemer

Father, Son... now Earthly Spirit! My system crucified, it rose again. This time in the hands of Englishmen – tough and fearless, ready for the fray. Nothing will stop them. Not even threats of deportation to Australia!

I explain to Caroline that I must return to London. She is heartbroken that we are to be parted once again, but knows where my heart lies.

He takes off his jacket.

'The Crisis' is upon us. That's what I call my newspaper. They have their 'Times', we have our 'Crisis'. Three hundred co-operative societies! In every town you could imagine. Listen! From the Armagh Co-operative Society: 'Dear Mr Owen, the supreme merit is yours, of devising a plan at once effectual, simple and stupendous....'

From the British Co-operative Magazine: 'Dear Mr Owen, we look to you as our founder and our teacher....'

From the London Co-operative Magazine: 'Dear Mr Owen, there is a growing affection and brotherly love every day more manifest amongst our members....'

'September 30th, 1830. Dearest Robert, still we cannot find a house to suit us. If I am to live within my income, I cannot afford a higher rent than thirty pounds a year. Our daughter Anne is very poorly, and the doctor views her condition with seriousness... my dear husband, how much I feel the want of your advice in a time of so much anxiety. My sincere wish is that nothing may ever happen to diminish this affection. Your loving wife, Caroline.'

He takes off his glasses.

I long to return to Lanark, but it is treachery to do so. The people demand that I address their meetings. In London, Bradford and in Manchester. I see their eyes intent upon me. They listen to my every word as if their lives depend upon it. Perhaps they do!

The army stands by as a million join my union in a few short months and march on Parliament! What can I do? Desert them as the hour strikes? I send letters home... and a little... more money. But the movement is consuming my resources, and my time, consuming me.

My dear daughter, Anne, is taken from me. I am distraught and desolate. Anne had been my favourite. A teacher in my schools. My comrade in the cause, well-read in all our schemes and our philosophy.

I return to Scotland. I go on foot in search of my lost family and I am shocked by their condition when I find them. They have barely space to live and yet the model of my village still holds pride of place. Jane is... cool towards me.

'How do you like our new society, Papa?' she asks. I answer that we strive to build a better world. 'For whom?' she says, 'For whom, Papa?' 'For all', I answer her. 'For all? Well, my society is here!' she scathes me. 'This house, this home, this family is where my duty lies!' 'Why, then, you are trapped by that which traps all womankind.' My wife and Mary, little Mary, die shortly after. Jane nurses them until the end.

He undoes his waistcoat.

England is on fire with rebellion! The Government is terrified and grants reform. But still the people press for more. They burn down the workhouses and riot in the streets, but they have no vision of a new society. Old man Owen is put out to grass. New leaders now arise. Oh, they are forthright enough. They are tough and brave.

197

They brim with confidence. But they have no strategy for a new order. In the end they settle for employment, for wages and the right to vote another set of tyrants into power. Not what I had in mind at all!

How the circle of my friends diminishes! The Lion – Doherty from Lancashire, Joe Harrison, and Smith the Shepherd. We... quarrel. Corrupted by the Church they are, in search of heaven hereafter. 'To hell with Owen's grand designs! Step by step!' But with each step the celestial city stretches further from their grasp. At first – an aim. It then becomes a dream. At last, a memory of some benign intentions of our boisterous youth.

Not for me – the millennium by installments! Not for me! No thank you, gentlemen! The heavens below, or not at all! No compromises. Society must be remade from top to bottom. And if man cannot remake it – remake man!

He takes off his shoes.

Fade.

Scene Six – The World of the Spirits

Owen sits in the chair, contemplative.

Well. I have my sons. They prosper. In America. But Mary, Anne and Caroline. I'll not see them again. The Church blames me for their deaths. They said, in fighting for humanity I'd sacrificed my own... become a cipher wedded to that frigid wife... a cause.

Is not the cause just? The principles – aren't they above reproach? The vision spotless? The banner, bright?

Well? Do the lives of orphan children weigh less in the scales of universal justice? God damn the Church! Caroline, Caroline. Forgive me!

You never flinched. You were steadfast to my cause, even through the years of my neglect. Oh yes, it was neglect. I could hide it from myself perhaps, but not from you, not now, at this late hour of my barren pilgrimage.

My accusers in the Church will tell you that they can love their fellows, yet love God more; love their wives and children yet love God more; love humanity but love God more. But they deny me that right because my faith is earthbound. Here, in this short span of breathing, living, being.

He pulls down his nightshirt.

I do not believe in the 'eternity' beyond, but, that hasn't stopped me going to see a spiritualist to make my peace with Caroline! A Mrs Hayden, an American. She wanted paying of course – she has to make a living. I asked if Caroline was at peace with herself? There came the reply that only our separation marred the sublime repose of her condition. But that was ever Caroline.

He wraps the blanket around himself.

Of late, my socialism has not been as popular as I would have wished. Those faithful to the cause still gather of a Sunday in my Temples of Science and Truth to preserve the message... keep it burning in their hearts. We hold a 'social' service and sing... 'social' hymns.

To the tune of 'There is a Green Hill Far Away':

'Community is labour bless'd
Redemption from the Fall.
The good of all by each possess'd
the good of each by all.'

Then, I read the 'social sermon'. Sometimes I bless the children of my flock Matthew, Mark, Ernest, Arthur. And we take a collection to pay the wages of our socialist missionaries, ordained by me, who travel forth to towns and mills and factories. Well? Is there a better way? It is what people have grown used to over a thousand years.

They make such a fuss of me. Whenever I enter the temples, the socialists all stand up, stand up – for me. Me! They set me in a chair and offer a towel for me to wipe my face.

When I finished my last meeting in Liverpool, I was lifted from the platform and carried slowly out whilst the congregation stood. Some reached out to touch my clothing as I passed. One young child said 'Is that Jesus, mother?'

'God Bless you, Mr Owen', the voices came. God Bless me? I don't know how to take that. Take it in the right spirit I suppose, as it was meant.

He holds his heart.

Well. There's a pain for you! Under socialism, we'll abolish pain and – that's just for a start!

Mrs Williams! Where is the woman? Not gone to fetch a priest, I trust? That would do my heart no good at all! I have enough problems and tomorrow is a busy day.

Oh, how time eats into the paltry agenda of our schemes! Blink! A decade passes. A fortune won and squandered. Blink! Another gone. A bold experiment that fired the vision of a continent is abandoned, overgrown with weeds. Blink! An army of redress once proud and confident is scattered into lonely rooms where old men drivel stories of the dreams of childhood.

I've failed, you know! I've nothing now to show. A crank! A relic from the age of optimists. An old Welsh wizard weaving legends from the wings of bats and night-jars, concocting elixirs to wash away the warts from the fingers of vagabonds and beggars.

I could have had a life of ease and comfort, shut off from the trials and struggles of our people.

'Dear old Owen, what a character! He became incredibly rich, went raving mad and then became a socialist.'

But from where I stood, the world went mad. I simply went in search of sanity. Call it a vision. Call it a dream. But, oh, the power of a dream. It is more potent than this small frame, this feeble flesh and blood.

In dreams we live; in dreams endure.

I have a sense of something abiding in the human spirit; a true communion that binds each man and woman to a greater purpose than our dismal vanities, our selfish strivings.

It is as if New Town, New Lanark and New Harmony are merely footsteps on a journey to a New World, which we will come upon when we least expect it, when all seems lost and it becomes essential. Oh yes, it has to come.

Mrs Williams! The fire, Mrs Williams. The fire must not go out!

Spotlight on Owen fades to darkness.

The End.

NORA'S BLOKE

Original Cast

Narrator/Mikey - Toby Harris
Cathy James - Roisin Clancy-Davies
Deidre Mahoney - Julie-Ann Dean
Molly Stack - Marie-Claire Costley
Nora O'Rourke - Gwynyfa Bawler
Lottie Mutton - Liz Edney
Nathan Blumberg - Simon Futty
Grandmother James - Gill Rees

With special thanks to Sian Bundy, Cardiff Everyman Theatre, Katherine O'Sullivan and Leslie Hoban Blake at the Blue Heron Theatre, New York City

ACT ONE
Prologue

To the slow movement of Mozart's clarinet concerto – the signature tune of the play – the stage lightens. It is a dull day. There is a battered table and chairs centre stage, an old piano against the back wall, on top of it a crackling wireless. The kitchen is off-stage back left and there is a window front stage left. Rear right is the door leading to the landing and there is another door stage right, to the only bedroom. A worse-for-wear sofa is right, at right angles to the footlights. We can imagine the fireplace front centre stage. Two low footstools are either side of it. Enter NARRATOR/MIKEY casually surveying the scene, a traveller from the future, returned to scenes of the past.

NARRATOR/MIKEY: You can never return to those childhood places, except as a ghost from a life yet to be lived. This is the place. A one-bedroom flat on the first floor of number one hundred and six, St Thomas's Road, Finsbury Park, London N4, England, Great Britain, on the planet Earth, in the solar system, somewhere in space.

Outside these four walls, a world war was raging – bombs, guided missiles, searchlights, anti-aircraft guns. Inside, my mother cleared a space for my childhood games. Legions of Irishwomen would drink tea around this table late into the night as I sat listening underneath. They also played games of their own. Secret games I wasn't supposed to know about.

Enter CATHY, zombie-like. She sits at a table.

NARRATOR/MIKEY: Where's Dad, Mam? Will he come back? When?

CATHY stares into space, cut off by time. Her head turns but she does not hear.

NARRATOR/MIKEY: My mother didn't know when. None of us knew. We lived for the next piece of toast; the next air-raid; the next letter from the front; and the next Irishwoman to come through the door. Speak to me, Ma! Make them all come alive!

CATHY activates and becomes a living person. Even when she appears to scold, she is smiling with it.

CATHY: Look at the time, child! It's midnight! For God's sake go to bed!

NARRATOR/MIKEY: No, Mam. There's a banshee in the bedroom! It's combing its hair and laughing like a witch!

CATHY: A banshee? Nonsense! Who told you that?

NARRATOR/MIKEY: You did. I heard you telling Deidre.

CATHY: Ah, it was just a story. You're seven years old! Away to bed, while Deidre and I have a cup of tea.

NARRATOR/MIKEY: Deidre Mahoney, streetwise but superstitious – my mother's best friend.

Enter DEIDRE.

DEIDRE: Come here Mikey, till I tell you. (*Loud whisper.*) Did you know the Queen has a golden toilet seat that goes everywhere with her?

NARRATOR/MIKEY: What for, Auntie Deidre?

DEIDRE: So if she wants a royal pee, the royal arse won't be infected by the likes of you and me.

NARRATOR/MIKEY: Is it real gold?

DEIDRE: Solid, Mikey. Solid! And do you know what King George does for a livin'? He sits all day on his throne eatin' bananas from a silver tray!

NARRATOR/MIKEY: What's a banana, Auntie Deidre?

DEIDRE: Ask your Auntie Molly. She knows all about bananas.

NARRATOR/MIKEY: Ah yes, Molly – part bohemian, part school-marm. And other things besides.

DEIDRE links arms on CATHY's left. Enter MOLLY, dressed in trousers, double-breasted jacket with cravat and a trilby hat. She smokes a cigarette in a long holder and approaches NARRATOR/ MIKEY. Perhaps NARRATOR/MIKEY kisses MOLLY, as if greeting an old, living friend.

MOLLY: A banana, child, is a very dirty kind of fruit.

MIKEY: But the King eats them!

MOLLY (*grimaces*): Ah, don't! The very thought of it!

MOLLY links arms with CATHY on her right, in front of the table.

NARRATOR/MIKEY: Molly Stack worked in the cloakroom of a posh night club. I thought she stole the men's clothes to wear. And then there was Lottie Mutton, our cockney landlady, from downstairs. The weight of the world was on Lottie.

LOTTIE, in pinafore and headscarf, leans on the door-frame, glumly smoking a dog-end. The three Irishwomen all turn.

LOTTIE: Oh! Full 'ouse tonight? Wassis 'en? IRA meetin'?

DEIDRE (*with wicked irony*): Ah Mrs Mutton, you've a sharp sense of humour! Hasn't she, so?

MOLLY (*languidly*): You're a laugh a minute, Lottie.

LOTTIE: 'Ere Kaff! Your mate, wassername, Nora, the wicked witch, called yesterday. Knocked so loud she woke Big Ern up... and 'e's on nights! Have a word wiv' her!

Exit LOTTIE.

CATHY: Will you listen to her! Bombs droppin' all around and Ern gets woken by a knock on the door!

NARRATOR/MIKEY: But the queen of them all was Nora, a woman so ugly that it used to keep me awake at nights. I thought Nora was the banshee.

CATHY: Ah! Poor Nora!

DEIDRE: Ah! Sure God help her!

MOLLY: What was your man, God, thinking of when he put that poor woman together!

CATHY: God has a wicked sense of humour!

DEIDRE: Mind you, she has a heart o' Gold!

CATHY and MOLLY: Oh a heart o' gold! She'd give you her last penny.

CATHY starts a laughing fit. MOLLY and DEIDRE help her to a chair.

CATHY: Oh God, I'll die, sure I will!

DEIDRE: Quiet. She's in the kitchen. She'll hear you!

CATHY: Come and join us, Nora!

NORA (*loudly, off from kitchen*): No. Youse'll all be laughin' at me!

ALL: Ah, we won't. We won't!

MOLLY: We promise not to laugh. Will we, girls?

CATHY struggles to cover laughter.

NORA (*shouting, defiantly, from kitchen*): I only have one wish in this world and that's a nice bloke to marry me. Is that too much to be asking?

CATHY, DEIDRE and MOLLY whisper amongst themselves.

CATHY: That's a tough one!

MOLLY: One day, she'll meet 'Mr Right'!

CATHY: 'Mr Right!' Can you imagine the state of him?

NORA (*voice off, defiantly*): I'd be a good catch for any man! I'm a de-cent res-pect-able gerrul! What am I?

CATHY, DEIDRE and MOLLY: You're a de-cent res-pect-able gerrul!

Fade.

Scene One – The Home Front

August, 1944. Weekday, late afternoon. The stage is in darkness. The lights go up very gradually, but never very bright. Between scenes, a news broadcast comes, not from the wireless, but from the ether, as the lights go up.

NEWSREADER: This is the BBC Home Service for today, August the twenty-second, 1944. During the night, three German V1 flying bombs caused minor damage in agricultural areas in Kent and Sussex. Ninety-two were destroyed by RAF Spitfires before they could reach their targets. The first of eight new deep shelters has been opened...

An air raid warning siren starts up, a wailing sound rising and falling in pitch. NARRATOR/MIKEY rushes in, holding a tennis ball. The sound of a flying bomb is heard, spluttering across the sky. He runs to the blacked-out window and peeps out, excitedly, without fear. Anti-aircraft batteries start up. Suddenly the flying bomb's engine cuts out. All Londoners knew this meant the bomb was falling and could calculate impact by a few simple rules. Enter CATHY, out of breath, shouting urgently. She drops her shopping bag, grabs NARRATOR/MIKEY's arm and pushes him towards the table.

CATHY: Mikey! Mikey, quick! Get in there under the table!

NARRATOR/MIKEY drops the ball and goes to retrieve it.

CATHY: Never mind the bloody ball.

They scramble under the table, facing stage front. After a short silence, an explosion rocks the house.

NARRATOR/MIKEY: Can I get my ball now?

CATHY: And how'll you play football with no legs on you? Here comes another one. See! Didn't I tell you!

CATHY closes her eyes and sticks her fingers in her ears. MIKEY crawls out to retrieve the ball.

CATHY: Mikey! Come here till I kill you!

NARRATOR/MIKEY scampers back with ball. CATHY embraces his head, protecting it. Another explosion.

NARRATOR/MIKEY: The newsman said no rockets reach London, Mam.

CATHY: Well what was that, then? Jelly and custard?

NARRATOR/MIKEY: But he said!

CATHY: If he said Father Christmas was a black man, would you believe him?

NARRATOR/MIKEY: How do the rockets know where to go?

CATHY: Electrics! Them Germans are awful clever with electrics.

NARRATOR/MIKEY: Perhaps the pilot jumps off at the last minute. Then parachute. Eeeeeeeaaaa! Bump! Then I could capture him and swap him for Daddy.

CATHY: That's a great idea. Why didn't I think of that?

NARRATOR/MIKEY: Do the Germans give Daddy food?

CATHY: Nothin' fancy! A sausage and a bit of bread.

NARRATOR/MIKEY: Well if they give Daddy food, why are they nasty?

CATHY: 'Nazis' darlin', 'Nazis'. But it's the same thing.

NARRATOR/MIKEY: Mam, how can you trap Germans in a handkerchief?

CATHY: Mikey, what the devil are you talking about?

NARRATOR/MIKEY: Well on that poster in the underground it says 'Trap the Germans in your handkerchief!'

CATHY: 'Germs', darlin', not Germans. Little tiny things that spread diseases.

NARRATOR/MIKEY: Mam! What will all the Daddies do when the war's over?

CATHY: They'll go to work, of course.

NARRATOR/MIKEY: No, no. I mean who will they fight against?

CATHY embraces him and kisses his cheek.

CATHY: Ah, the poor child. You've never known anything else but war and bombs and hiding under tables. Give Mammy a kiss.

The all-clear siren sounds. Approaching footsteps can be heard, of DEIDRE and MOLLY descending the stairs from Deidre's upstairs flat.

DEIDRE (*voice off*): There's a light on. Thank God they're back.

CATHY: Quick now, here come the girls. Wash your hands and face and I'll be there to tuck you in.

NARRATOR/MIKEY: But Ma! I want to hear the stories.

CATHY: No arguments! You can listen at the door like you always do!

Fade.

Scene Two – Reading the Tea-Leaves

Evening, some weeks later. CATHY sits alone in a dim gas-lit room, reading a letter. The slow movement of Mozart's clarinet concerto can be heard on the wireless. The VOICE is that of her prisoner of war husband, David.

DAVID'S VOICE (*voice off*): Dear Cath, I hope this letter reaches you and Mikey's safe and sound. I read your last letter over and over again, a dozen times a day sometimes, looking for the things you never say. I can't believe that Mikey will soon be eight. I know life was not much fun for you before all this and I was not always the best of men, but it's going to be different. I promise....

Enter DEIDRE.

DEIDRE: A letter?

CATHY: An old one.

DEIDRE: That last bomb was awful close. Yesterday they hit Copenhagen Street – not a house left standing. Can you not switch off Mozart's lavatory music? Drives me round the bend.

CATHY obliges. The wireless is on the piano.

CATHY: There's tea in the pot.

DEIDRE: A drop of cold water in mine to drink it quickly! Then you can read me fortune. I swear you're a genius with the tea-leaves.

CATHY comes in from the kitchen, with the tea cups.

DEIDRE: Listen, I've a favour to ask. Friday week, can you look after Brian and Theresa for me?

CATHY: What are you up to now?

DEIDRE: A little celebration. My wedding anniversary.

CATHY: Oh! Is Eddie coming home on leave?

DEIDRE: No. Listen till I tell you. This fellah, Joe, from the American Legion.

CATHY: Not another one!

DEIDRE: He's gorgeous. And you'd never guess. It's his wedding anniversary on the same day.

CATHY: Yes but to a different woman, Deidre! Anniversary! He could be making it all up!

DEIDRE: Cathy! I know he's making it up!

CATHY: God you're ruthless!

DEIDRE (*bubbling*): It's just like the theatre! I play his wife and he plays Eddie's part... if you get my meaning!

CATHY: Sounds like a bedroom farce to me.

DEIDRE: There's me tea finished. Right I'm closing my eyes. Swill the cup round three times, slowly. And there!

DEIDRE turns the cup upside down on the saucer. She opens her eyes. CATHY picks up the cup solemnly and places it on the palm of her hand, turning it slowly, staring at the tea-leaves intently.

CATHY: Mmmh! Yes. Aha!

DEIDRE (*excited*): Never mind the mmh-ah! What do you see?

CATHY: Shush, don't rush me. The pictures are forming in my mind.

DEIDRE: Cathy, do tea-leaves speak the truth?

CATHY: Tea-leaves never lie. Hush now. There's this great big rambling place with ivy leaves all around the windows, and the moon is shining on them as they rustle in the wind. The letter 'J'.

DEIDRE: That's Joe. He's taking me to an old hotel out somewhere in the country.

CATHY: Who's telling this fortune? Ah! There's a table set for two. Two plates on it. Wait now, it's not a table but a bed with two pillows.

DEIDRE (*keen*): Perhaps it's both. Perhaps we'll have a damn good steak first. What do you think?

CATHY: You're right. The square table is also a bed and the plates are pillows too.

DEIDRE: Thank God! I'm useless on an empty stomach.

CATHY: Hang on, now. There's an 'E' here, too. Yes, under the bed there's definitely an 'E'!

DEIDRE (*puts hand to her mouth*): It's my Eddie! What's Eddie doing there? He'd kill me if he found out.

CATHY: No the 'E' is not angry. He's in a reclining position, like he's asleep or something.

DEIDRE (*stands up*): What's happened to Eddie? Is he wounded? Poor Eddie! God forgive me! (*She sits.*)

CATHY: Wait now. No no no. It's nothing like that. Trust me. Have I ever been wrong yet? I see now what it is. It is an 'E', but from another angle it's a child's cot or a cradle or something. Yes.

DEIDRE (*stands up, walks around agitated*): Jesus! A cradle? That's even worse! Is there anything in the cradle? Like, a baby?

CATHY: I can't see inside the cradle. It's like half a baby. It's there and when I look again – not there.

DEIDRE (*sits*): It's a warning to me to be careful.

CATHY: Wait, there's more. A wedding or engagement or something. See, a ring with diamonds!

DEIDRE: Be God! And I'm not even divorced yet! Put it away, too much of a storm in that teacup! Cathy, why don't you make up a foursome. Joe's got a friend – Leo. The quiet type. Reads books.

CATHY: No I couldn't be doing that! Ask Molly!

DEIDRE: What? With her trousers and her Trilby hat? She has to think twice before using the ladies bog!

CATHY: Take Nora, then?

DEIDRE: Cathy, these poor men risk death every night on bombing raids! Their nerves are shot to pieces! They don't need Nora! Come on, have a bit of fun!

CATHY: Oh all right then. Just this once! Leo, you say?

DEIDRE: You'll love him! Friday week, then! We'll get Molly to babysit.

Fade.

Scene Three – Night Life

Two weeks later. LOTTIE glides in silently, wearing pinafore and headscarf, looking trance-like. She shuffles speedily to the kitchen area and looks in nervously. Just then, MOLLY enters quietly from the bedroom.

MOLLY: Mrs Mutton?

LOTTIE is startled and wheels around quickly, holding her heart.

LOTTIE: Oh! Oh! Wondered who you was, there, for a moment!

MOLLY: Mrs Mutton? You look a bit shaken.

LOTTIE: No. I'm all right. Big Ern's on the Scotland run again, and Doris is stayin' with her auntie. So I'm on me own.

MOLLY: Sit down a minute. Catherine's gone out with Deidre, to the... pictures. I'm babysitting. Sit down a minute for a chat.

LOTTIE (*backs towards the door*): It don't matter. Really it don't. I just thought I saw my brother come in here.

MOLLY: Your brother?

LOTTIE: Yeah. He was standin' at the top of the stairs and he beckoned me in 'ere. Wanted to talk, I reckon.

MOLLY: I didn't even know you had a brother.

LOTTIE: This used to be his bedroom, when we was kids. This is his watch I'm wearing. See? Stopped at ten past one.

MOLLY: I'm sorry, Lottie. This doesn't make any sense.

LOTTIE: Killed on the tenth of November 1918. In France it was. The last day of the war. He was just eighteen.

MOLLY: You mean he's dead? But...

LOTTIE: Not for me he ain't, though. I never could accept it. And whose turn will it be next, ay? My Little Ern had to register today, for his call up. 'E's eighteen, you see. That's the age. That's when it 'appened to our Tommy.

MOLLY: Lottie, have some tea. Have you been out at all, today?

LOTTIE: Out? I never goes out, not unless I really have to. I get this... funny feelin' when I goes out, like there's... too much space.

216

MOLLY: Have you not spoken to anyone about it? Your doctor?

LOTTIE: Nah! What do they know? Anyway. Gotta go. Gotta get little Ern's dinner. Late finish tonight.

MOLLY: Are you sure, now?

MOLLY sees her to the door. MOLLY looks spooked. Sits. Glances around nervously. Tries to read the paper. Knock on the door. Enter DEIDRE.

MOLLY: Oh it's you. Did you see Lottie on your way up?

DEIDRE: Walked right past me, like a bloody ghost. As usual! Not a word!

MOLLY: She's a troubled woman, Deidre. You should...

DEIDRE: Ah to hell with her! Anyway, just my bloody luck. Joe got called out on a mission! No date!

MOLLY: Where's Catherine, then?

DEIDRE: Livin' the life of Riley! My date it was, and she ends up with Leo at 'the the-atre', if you please, to see Laurence Olivier.

MOLLY: How nice? What's the show?

DEIDRE (*humourously; without malice*): Richard the bloody Fifth or somethin'. That Shakespeare mullarkey! Leo invited me too.

MOLLY: You should have gone!

DEIDRE: Shakespeare, on me wedding anniversary! Anyway! You're free to go Molly. I'll take over here.

MOLLY: No it's OK. I'll wait till Catherine gets back.

DEIDRE: You'll not see Cathy this side of breakfast! Them two are a fine pair o' ones! Like this they were. (*She makes chattering signs.*)

She was givin' him Charlotte bloody Bronte and Mozart and all the arty-farty.

MOLLY: Well, I just hope you know what you've started, Deidre Mahoney. There's no tellin' where this will end!

Fade.

Scene Four – The Madness of Cockneys

CATHY, DEIDRE and MOLLY are at the table. There is a knock at the door. LOTTIE pushes the door open and stands there, glumly leaning on the door-frame as she always does. She never comes into the room. A fag-end dangles from her mouth. She wears an apron and a scarf turban with curlers. In her hands: a dry mop. CATHY and DEIDRE are jiving to Glenn Miller.

LOTTIE: 'Allo gells.

CATHY: Mrs Mutton. I'll have the rent for you tomorrow. I missed the post office for me army allowance, what with the air raid, you know?

LOTTIE: Tomorrow will do. Bad news, Kaff. Little Ern got his call-up papers today. I don' want him to go, really I don't.

DEIDRE: Tell him to hop on the boat to Ireland. He'll be safe enough there.

LOTTIE: Big Ern says 'no'. It's his duty. I just hope it's the artillery, like his Dad. I don' want him in the infantry. And what's your lot playin' at over there? Why ain't they fightin' 'Itler with us?

DEIDRE: What d'you mean? The British army's choc-a-bloc with Paddies. My Eddie, for a start. It's the only work he could get.

LOTTIE: Yeah, but your bloke, Dellyvera, whatever 'is name is. He's well out of it, ain't 'e?

MOLLY: Ah, wait now. Mr De Valera has good reason for neutrality.

LOTTIE: Neutrality! 'Itler's a bleedin' maniac!

DEIDRE: That fellah gives me the creeps with his rantin' and ravin'! If you ask me, he's round the bend!

MOLLY: We're all agreed there, Mrs Mutton!

LOTTIE: No. It ain't just 'Itler. It's all the bloody Germans! Know what I'd do, if I had my way? Put 'em all up against the wall and shoot the bastards! Every single man-jack of 'em! For what they done to my family.

There is an uneasy silence.

CATHY (*softly*): Isn't war just an awful thing – what it does to us. When Mozart is playing on the wireless, the slow movement of the clarinet concerto, it's so beautiful I think my heart will burst with the sadness of it. And I think, how can a people who produced such a fine, fine man, how could they have sunk so low?

MOLLY: Did you know what Mozart's middle name was? Amadeus. 'Loved by God.'

CATHY: Really? Now isn't that strange? For I often think think that one day the Germans will realise they all have a bit of Mozart in them, especially when I hear that heart-rending solo in the second movement.

DEIDRE (*lightening the proceedings*): Personally I'd shoot Mozart first, just for that! Hey, Mozart! Front of the queue!

Laughter all round, including LOTTIE.

MOLLY: Deidre, you're a barbarian!

CATHY: Isn't she just?

DEIDRE: It's Glenn Miller for me, every time!

CATHY: Anyway Lottie, not to worry. They say it could all be over by Christmas.

LOTTIE: They said that last Christmas and the Christmas before. I dunno, really I don't. We're supposed to be winning, but these bombs get worse all the time.

DEIDRE: To listen to the news you'd think it was bloody Palm Beach here, not rockets and whole streets being flattened.

LOTTIE: They have to say that, don't they. For the people up North. (*Miserably.*) It keeps up our morale! 'Ere Kaff! Tell Mikey to wipe 'is feet. This is the second time I've done the stairs today.

CATHY: I will. I will. Good night Mrs Mutton.

LOTTIE: I'll be orf then!

Exit Lottie.

DEIDRE: Isn't she the miserablest old ghet!

CATHY (*whispering*): Wait now, she could be listening at the door. (*Walks to door. Shouts loudly, for effect.*) Ah, she's a decent old stick, really. We'd have been on the streets if it wasn't for good old Lottie. (*Pause.*) It's all right. She's gone! Never argue with her, Molly, or me and Deidre could be out on the street.

MOLLY: I was only standing up for my own country.

DEIDRE: Listen Molly, that woman doesn't give a damn for the Irish. It's only the rent she's after from us.

MOLLY: Sorry I spoke.

CATHY: And they don't need it. Four wage packets coming in. Herself and Doris. Big Ern's on the railways and Little Ern at the bakery.

DEIDRE: And him a great ox of a lad like his father! And the pair of us with two husbands away fightin' for King and Country. Her

King. Her country!

CATHY (*confiding*): D'ye know she polishes that lino like a mad thing. Last week I nearly broke me neck sliding the whole length of the stairs. Shopping, the lot!

DEIDRE: Well I'm glad Little Ern's been called up. It's not as if he has a wife and family.

CATHY: She's not right in the head, you know. It's well known one in five cockneys are half-mad. And the other four are OK, so it must be her!

MOLLY (*calmly*): Did you know she lost a brother in the last war? It was on the last day.

CATHY: She's never said a word to me about it.

DEIDRE: Me neither, all the time I've known her.

MOLLY (*tiring of the gossip*): I shouldn't imagine that's done much for her sanity. Well, I've some shopping to do. I can see you two have things to talk about. So long!

CATHY and DEIDRE: So long, Molly!

Exit MOLLY.

CATHY: That was a sharp exit. Is she in a mood or something?

DEIDRE: Who gives a damn? So you're hitting it off with Leo! That's great!

CATHY: Sshh! Mikey will hear you!

DEIDRE: Didn't I tell you you would. Joe says he's absolutely mad about you. Talks about you all the time!

CATHY: He's getting too serious.

DEIDRE: Ah just make the most of it while it lasts.

CATHY: But I'm not like you, Deidre. I get serious too!

DEIDRE: Give yourself a bit of space. Can you not send Mikey down to Wales with his grannie for a week or two?

CATHY: I might have to. Caledonian Road got hit again last night, and the railway yards at Finsbury Park.

Fade.

Scene Five – Fear and Loathing in Caerfarchell

NARRATOR/MIKEY walks to front of a suddenly darkened stage, dimly lit where he pulls a mattress out from the wings. Next to the mattress is a small, low table. On the table is a spotlighted stuffed owl in a glass case.

NARRATOR/MIKEY: And that's how it was. When the V1 rockets got worse, I'd be put on the train at Paddington and collected by 'Mamma' – my Welsh grandmother, who lived in a remote cottage on the edge of a misty moor in the far, far west of Wales, by the cliffs of the Atlantic Ocean.

NARRATOR/MIKEY gets on to the mattress, covers himself with a blanket and stares, terrified, at the owl.

NARRATOR/MIKEY: Mamma! Mamma! Come quickly!

Enter MAMMA, his Welsh grandmother, old, stooped and trudging, carrying a candlestick.

GRANDMOTHER: What is it with you, now, boy?

NARRATOR/MIKEY: The owl! It's eyes are moving!

GRANDMOTHER (*peers through the glass*): Don't be daft, mun! Glass eyes, they are!

NARRATOR/MIKEY: It comes alive at night and flies around the room!

GRANDMOTHER: No. No. Dead it is, mun. Dead these fifty years, to my knowledge! (*She knocks hard on the glass.*)

NARRATOR/MIKEY (*jumps, fearfully*): Can't we bury it then?

GRANDMOTHER: Bury it? Then what's for to keep you company in the daaark?

She begins to trudge away, chuckling to herself.

NARRATOR/MIKEY: Mamma! What's for dinner tomorrow?

GRANDMOTHER: Same as today.

NARRATOR/MIKEY: Parsley soup with bones?

GRANDMOTHER: To sleep with you, now!

NARRATOR/MIKEY (*glancing at owl and trying to delay her departure*): And Mamma, what's... the name... of Mr James' sheepdog?

GRANDMOTHER (*stops in her tracks, to think*): Duw! Duw! You've got me there! What is the creature's name? Wait a minute now, it'll come to me. Ah yes.

NARRATOR/MIKEY: What is it then?

GRANDMOTHER: 'Doggy!' is 'is name. Aye, that's it. 'Doggy.'

NARRATOR/MIKEY: That's not a very good name.

GRANDMOTHER (*chuckles*): Well it's not a very good dog.

NARRATOR/MIKEY: Is his full name... 'Doggy James', then?

GRANDMOTHER (*irritated*): Why do you want to know?

NARRATOR/MIKEY: For when I call him, of course!

GRANDMOTHER: The dog only answers to his master's whistling.

NARRATOR/MIKEY: Mamma, when I throw sticks for him to fetch, he just sits there and doesn't do nothing.

GRANDMOTHER: Sticks, indeed! Why you throwin' sticks, then?

NARRATOR/MIKEY: You know, playing with him!

GRANDMOTHER: Playin'? Playin'? Don't you never play with that dog. A workin' dog, he is. Spoil 'im you will and he'll be no good for to fetch the sheep.

GRANDMOTHER *heads off. Again, MIKEY tries to delay her, glancing at the owl.*

NARRATOR/MIKEY: Mamma?

GRANDMOTHER: What now? I've work to do in the scullery!

NARRATOR/MIKEY: When you throw the soup bones away...

GRANDMOTHER: Throw them away! Diolch! There's two more days goodness in them!

NARRATOR/MIKEY: Yes, but when you do throw them, can I have them, please?

GRANDMOTHER: What for do you want them ol' bones?

NARRATOR/MIKEY: For Doggy James. I think he's hungry.

GRANDMOTHER: I should hope he is, too! A hungry dog will work for you. Feed him, indeed! I can't be keeping the neighbours dogs in bones! There's a war on! Let him eat his master's sheep, if he must.

NARRATOR/MIKEY: Mamma? Can I...

GRANDMOTHER: All these questions!

NARRATOR/MIKEY: Can I have some bread and cheese?

GRANDMOTHER: What do you say, then?

NARRATOR/MIKEY: Please?

GRANDMOTHER: No. You can't. Eating at night makes you have dreams. God forbid!

NARRATOR/MIKEY: I won't dream, honestly.

GRANDMOTHER: I should hope not, neither! Good night to you.

NARRATOR/MIKEY: Mamma! Did Daddy used to sleep in this bed?

GRANDMOTHER: Three of them slept by yere, and the other four down by there.

NARRATOR/MIKEY: Gosh! That's a lot.

GRANDMOTHER: Aye, a lot it was. And if they didn't go to sleep, their father would have the belt to them! Lucky you are that he's not yere now, or he'd do the same to you.

NARRATOR/MIKEY: What happened to him? Where is he?

GRANDMOTHER: Died he did, ten long years ago. Just over by there, in the corner. All skin and bone he was!

NARRATOR/MIKEY: Is Daddy skin and bone, too?

GRANDMOTHER: A fine man, your father – big and strong. You'll meet him, soon enough! And then, watch out! There'll be no more galavanting around London for your mother!

NARRATOR/MIKEY: What's 'galavanting', Mamma?

GRANDMOTHER: Ask your mother when you gets home. She'll know!

NARRATOR/MIKEY(*excited*): Am I going home, then? When? Is it soon?

GRANDMOTHER: Next Friday. Nine o'clock train. And none too soon!

GRANDMOTHER departs with candle.

NARRATOR/MIKEY (*staring at the corner*): Mamma! Just a minute!

GRANDMOTHER (*voice off*): Is it a bedtime kiss you want with me?

GRANDMOTHER chuckles and departs as MIKEY turns the owl to face the wall and buries his head under the pillow. After she's left, MIKEY reappears as NARRATOR, pushing away the props.

NARRATOR/MIKEY: My Grandmother was canny. She had a large wart on her chin. With hairs on it. And she knew I hated to have to kiss it at bedtime. She was kind in her way. She would never actually allow me to die, but beyond that it was a matter of 'sink or swim'. All the same, Hitler had much to fear from her grim Protestant-Welsh virtues: hard graft, doggedness and a deep contempt for idle pleasures such as novels, plays and the cinema. With the money Cathy sent her for my food, she bought government war bonds. Oh yes! It takes all sorts to win a war. So, when the rocket raids eased off, Mamma would put me on a train at Haverfordwest with a bag containing one strangled chicken from her half-starved flock. She used to do the strangling herself, because it gave her pleasure. It was great to be back in London, where the searchlights lit up the skies, because I knew in my heart that if anyone could finish off Hitler, it was my mother and her cronies.

Fade.

Scene Six – Banshees of Various Types

Stage lightens on the flat. Evening. CATHY is writing a letter. Classical violin music is playing low on the wireless. CATHY reads through, making corrections.

CATHY (*voice over*): 'Dear David, don't worry about Mikey. He is at your mother's. He really loves it in Solva and Mamma's always so kind and generous. She feeds him well and he always comes back with rosy cheeks from the fresh air...'

Enter DEIDRE. She knocks and bursts in.

DEIDRE: Can you give me hair a trim? Oh, you're busy.

CATHY: No. Just a letter to David.

DEIDRE: Can you not switch off that awful row. It's like a cat going through a mangle? I think I heard Molly on her way up.

CATHY: I wish you hadn't told her about Leo. I know she doesn't approve.

CATHY switches off the Mozart. DEIDRE sits. CATHY throws a cloth around DEIDRE's shoulders and starts trimming. Both face the audience. Enter MOLLY. She never shortens names and is always very correct.

MOLLY: Hello Deidre. Hello Catherine.

DEIDRE: Well if it isn't Marlene Dietrich! No top hat and tails tonight, I see!

MOLLY: I have the day off. Here, Catherine, I bought this train set for Michael's birthday. Only one carriage, mind, and a circle of rails. (*Puts it on the table.*)

CATHY: Oh, he'll be delighted with that! Thanks.

DEIDRE: How's life at Angelo's?

MOLLY: The familiar story. Girls – absolutely throwing themselves at American officers.

DEIDRE: What a girl won't do for nylon stockings!

MOLLY: Nylons I can understand. It's what they have to submit to afterwards.

DEIDRE: Molly, 'submitting' is the best part. What are we all – nuns?

CATHY: Come on now Molly, have you never given the eye to a nice Yank, just the once?

MOLLY: You mean, a man?

DEIDRE: Of course she means a man.

MOLLY (*light-heartedly*): Catherine, I'd never believe we'd all spent twelve years in the same convent school.

CATHY: What are you getting at?

DEIDRE: Let's not go down that particular path, Cathy. We all get our pleasures in different ways. After twelve years of the Holy Mary, and the 'Blessed Virgin', I used to get horny just thinking about Jesus.

MOLLY: And to think I was going to ask if you'd come to Mass on Sunday.

DEIDRE: Ah, you wouldn't want to be in a long queue behind me at the confession box.

MOLLY: What about you, Catherine?

CATHY: David made me swear I'd never let Mikey set foot in a Catholic church. He says nuns are a queer breed. Man-haters the lot of 'em. He says they're all in love with Our Lady.

DEIDRE: Let's change the subject, shall we?

MOLLY: Come on! We're still all good Catholics!

CATHY: I am not!

MOLLY: But you must believe in something!

DEIDRE: She believes in tea-leaves.

CATHY: Yes, somewhere up there in the great blue yonder is a bloody great teapot that sits in judgement.

MOLLY: But why a teapot?

CATHY: Because it's got nothin' better to do!

MOLLY: You're codding me.

DEIDRE: She's not codding. This woman sees things you wouldn't believe. Don't start her off!

The haircutting finished, DEIDRE takes off the cloth and they all sit. CATHY takes a seat facing the door. DEIDRE and MOLLY with their backs to it. She begins to draw them in to her story and their heads draw closer together.

CATHY: Did I ever tell you...

DEIDRE: There! You've done it now, Molly.

CATHY: 'Twas not long after I'd left the convent. I'd gone back to Tramore to see an old friend and I took the short cut back from the Cove. It was the twilight, but I wasn't at all spooked or anything. I came to a stretch where the river tumbles over the rocks into a deep pool. And I could hear a faint song which seemed to come from beneath the water and then I saw the pool begin to brim...

At this point NORA, unseen by the others, enters and begins to steal towards the group quietly so as not to disturb the story. She shuffles in. She wears a long mac, thick horn-rimmed glasses, with hair down over her eyes. She smokes a fag. MOLLY and DEIDRE are totally entranced and unaware of her.

CATHY (*continuing*): I thought it might be an otter or something, but this kind of a hump began to surface and then the shoulders and then the head of a woman and her long hair, dripping with weeds. She was all in black and searching for something in the water. And I must have made some slight movement, for suddenly she swirled around and looked right into me. And then this voice called out...

NORA coughs loudly, from the cigarette. DEIDRE swings round to see NORA right behind her. She screams with fear and swoons.

DEIDRE: Aaaaaah. Oh God! God! Oh me heart!

NORA: Is it the banshee story? I've heard it!

MOLLY rushes to get a glass of water for DEIDRE, as CATHY prevents DEIDRE falling to the floor in a faint.

MOLLY: For God's sake, Nora did you have to creep up on us like that without a word?

CATHY takes the glass from MOLLY and feeds it to DEIDRE, who slowly comes round. NORA peers playfully into her face as her eyes open.

NORA: Whoowa! It's only me. Who did you think?

DEIDRE: Ah get away, Nora! You nearly frightened the life out of me.

NORA: I've a bag of fish and chips. Here, dip in! (*She places the bag on the table.*)

DEIDRE (*fanning herself*): Jesus, Nora. You should carry a bell after dark!

MOLLY: Well I have to say, Catherine, you spin an awful good yarn.

DEIDRE: Don't be takin' the mick. This woman has the powers of a bloody witch. Read Molly's tea-leaves for her.

MOLLY: No heathen stuff for me, I'll just have the tea.

NORA, stuffs chips into her mouth. The other three join the feast.

NORA: So what are youse all up to? Deidre? Any men on the scene?

MOLLY: My lips are sealed.

NORA: I promise I won't steal him from you. Does he have a friend?

DEIDRE: He has. A fellah named Leo.

NORA clasps her hands together, like an excited child.

NORA: Fix me up with a date!

DEIDRE: Nora! I don't do things like that to friends. Besides, he already has a girlfriend.

NORA *(juts out her chin)*: And who might that be?

Silence. DEIDRE looks at CATHY.

NORA: Oh! I see!

NORA stands up and walks to the window, looking out. The girls are embarrassed.

NORA: It doesn't matter. He doesn't sound like my type at all.

MOLLY: And what type would that be?

NORA: The marrying kind.

DEIDRE: Joe's married. I don't know about Leo.

NORA: Isn't that just typical? The two of them with a husband apiece and they're after two more. Is it any wonder a girl like me can't get a look in. Tell you what Molly, you and me will go out on the town and pick up a couple of fellahs.

DEIDRE: Molly doesn't fancy men, Nora.

NORA: At school she used to fancy Father O'Brien.

DEIDRE: Father O'Brien was an oul' he-she. He'd be after spending hours in the potting shed with Vincent the gardener, polishing the cucumbers.

NORA: Look, if you're shy, I'll do the talkin'! With your looks and my gab we'll be quids in. You can choose. I'll have the ugly one!

DEIDRE: But would the ugly one have you?

NORA rises haughtily and walks towards the door.

NORA: Looks aren't everything! Call yourselves friends! I know I'm no oil painting, but somewhere out there is a fellah, a decent fellah, and he's looking for a girl like me. If you won't help me find him, I'll find him myself. You're a selfish bunch of divils, so y'are! And you don't deserve the husbands you've got.

Exit NORA, in a huff. MOLLY tries to stop her.

CATHY: We've really put our foot in it this time. Poor Nora!

DEIDRE: Poor Nora, nothin'. She has to know the truth!

MOLLY: You've done nothin' but insult the woman all night!

DEIDRE: But you wouldn't be seen dead with her.

MOLLY: We've got to find him.

CATHY: Find who?

MOLLY: Nora's bloke. He's out there somewhere.

DEIDRE: But how are we to find him?

MOLLY: Let's just say... it's our contribution to the war effort.

CATHY: If you can find a bloke for Nora, Hitler's finished!

Fade.

Optional end of Act One.

Scene Seven – The Hidden Hand of Fate

Stage lightens. CATHY sits reading a letter from MIKEY.

NARRATOR/MIKEY (*voice over*): Dear Mammy, I hop you are weel. I made a camp in Mr James' haystack. Have the bombs stopped yet? Mama put an owl in my bedroom. She says it's dead and won't hurt me, but I think it's alive because its eyes move. Lots of love, Mikey.

LOTTIE taps on the door and lolls in the doorway.

LOTTIE: 'Ere Kaff, Little Ern's home on leave.

CATHY: That's great news. Didn't I tell you he'd be all right?

LOTTIE: He's finished his training. They put him in the Ulster Rifles but he ain't Irish.

CATHY: That's all right. Neither are they.

LOTTIE: He's gorn for a pint with Big Ern. The bad news is they're posting him abroad when he gets back. They won't say, but I reckon it's France. I don' like it, Kaff.

CATHY: Lottie, you mustn't be worrying yourself sick all day and night. Gerry's on his last legs.

Enter MOLLY.

MOLLY: Ah Mrs Mutton, I've just seen your husband and little Ern on their way to the Plimsoll Arms. And doesn't he look a fine, great, strapping lad in his uniform. You must be awful proud of him?

LOTTIE: Look at 'er in her men's clothes again. You wanna watch it gel, one of these days you'll get picked up by some tart.

MOLLY: We live in hope, Lottie. We live in hope.

LOTTIE: She's a right one, this gel! I must be orff! Bloody Germans!

Exit LOTTIE.

CATHY (*whispers*): God, you'd think she was the only one with a son in the war.

MOLLY: He is only eighteen.

CATHY: He's fit and strong. No wife or kid.

MOLLY: All the same. Her only son.

CATHY: I've no patience with the woman. Big Ern doing all the overtime God made. Trust a cockney to make money in wartime! They're rolling in it!

MOLLY: You're a bit hard on her.

CATHY: Hard? My David wasting away in a Nazi camp on bread and drippin'. Well, now she knows what it's like. About time too!

MOLLY: I'll not argue with you.

CATHY: No, don't! I'm not in the mood. I have a son, too. With an old hag of a grandmother, frightenin' the life out of him with owls! And what's to happen to David when the troops advance?

MOLLY: The Germans wouldn't shoot British prisoners. He'll be back. The question is, Cathy, do you want him back?

CATHY *bursts into tears.*

MOLLY (*puts an arm round her and offers a hanky*): Here. Go on. Take it.

CATHY: You know I've been stopping over. At Leo's.

MOLLY: I guessed as much.

CATHY (*angry with herself*): I feel so guilty!

MOLLY: So? You deserve a bit of happiness. God knows there isn't much of it about.

CATHY: Happiness? Do I look happy? (*Through her tears.*) What do you know about it, anyway. You've never been with a man in your life!

MOLLY: I can't help the way God made me.

CATHY (*still wiping the tears*): Oh shut up about God! You're just too bloody frightened to take a real man on.

MOLLY (*calmly*): I'm no stranger to sadness, Catherine.

CATHY: And what have you to be sad about?

MOLLY (*remains calm, dignified*): At least you've got someone. Me, I'm just an old misfit. It's a lonely life for the likes of me. If it wasn't for you and Deidre and Nora I'd go slowly round the bend.

CATHY (*remorsefully. She pulls herself together*): I'm sorry I was sharp with you. You're a good friend to me. To all of us. Mikey says thank you, for the train set.

MOLLY: I was going to by him a doll!

CATHY *smiles and cheers up.*

MOLLY: How's Nora? Have you seen Nora?

CATHY: She's not speaking to me, or Deidre.

Enter DEIDRE. Ironically, she makes the sign of the cross, like a priest.

DEIDRE: God save all here! Have you been crying, Cathy?

CATHY: Just a cold.

MOLLY signals for DEIDRE to leave it alone.

MOLLY: We were just talking about Nora. I hear she hasn't been around for weeks.

DEIDRE: She's probably hangin' upside down with the other bats.

CATHY: Ah leave the poor girl alone. It's not her fault.

MOLLY: I have a little plan, to help her find someone.

DEIDRE: You mean a human being?

MOLLY: Here. The Islington Gazette. Lonely Hearts.

DEIDRE: Desperate hearts more like it. All kinds of quare fellahs answer those things.

CATHY: What would be the cost of it?

MOLLY: Expensive. Penny-ha'penny a word.

DEIDRE: With Nora, the less said, the better.

MOLLY: Twelve words. One and sixpence. A tanner apiece? What do you say?

DEIDRE: Sixpence? Each!

CATHY: We owe it to Nora. Count me in!

MOLLY: Deidre?

DEIDRE: The words don't exist that could describe that woman. It's lies we'll have to tell. Bloody big ones!

MOLLY: Cathy, you're the one with the words.

CATHY: Well, let me see....

They wait in anticipation.

DEIDRE: Here. Gimme the pencil. I'll write it down.

CATHY: Well, she's a decent old stick.

MOLLY: Leave out 'old stick'. Just put 'decent'.

DEIDRE: 'Decent hag. Dyin' for a shag.' How's that!

MOLLY: Be serious now Deidre Mahoney.

DEIDRE: Yes, Miss!

MOLLY: What else is Nora O'Rourke?

CATHY: She's respectable. Wait now, what is it she always says...

ALL: Im a decent respectable gerrul!

CATHY: And it's true. Her own words.

DEIDRE (*writes*): 'Decent, respectable girl....'

CATHY: What else now. She has a fine pair of legs on her.

DEIDRE: Forty inch bust. They go for that! 'Forty inch bust with fine legs seeks short-sighted fellah.'

MOLLY: Will you forget legs and busts. The woman has a good heart.

CATHY: Yes, a 'heart of gold!'

MOLLY: Well done. A gold star for that one, Catherine.

DEIDRE (*writes*): Six words. Six to go.

CATHY: 'Seeks man for marriage and family.' Done!

MOLLY: Right enough. Read it out.

DEIDRE: 'Decent, respectable girl. Heart of Gold. Seeks man for marriage and family.' He'd have to be a desperado or a saint to answer that.

MOLLY: Come on then. Sixpence each, and not a word to Nora!

They hand the money to MOLLY.

Blackout.

Scene Eight – Finding Your Man

Inter-scene, we hear the news broadcast, voice over.

NEWSREADER (*voice over*): This is the BBC Home Service. Here is the nine o'clock news for today, Wednesday the twentieth of December. The German counter-offensive in the Ardennes forest of northern France continues to prevent Allied forces from making the final assault towards the Rhine....

Lights up.

CATHY sits at the table. DEIDRE walks around. A serious mood in the air.

DEIDRE: Are you sure you want to go through with this?

CATHY: I don't have a choice.

DEIDRE: There's adoption.

CATHY: I couldn't.

DEIDRE: Or an institution. The nuns?

CATHY: That was our childhood, Deidre. Would you want it for your own kids?

DEIDRE: I would not.

CATHY: Mikey would know. What would he think of me?

DEIDRE: Aren't you leaving someone out?

CATHY: You mean Leo?

DEIDRE: I mean you, Cathy.

CATHY: Oh, I'm the least of it!

DEIDRE: Not at all. What do you want in your own heart?

CATHY: Don't talk soft!

DEIDRE: Do you love him?

CATHY: David?

DEIDRE: Leo. Do you love Leo?

CATHY: I don't know what it is, but he cares about me in a way I've never known. The books I read. The music I listen to.

DEIDRE: Does he know?

CATHY: God, no. I haven't told him.

DEIDRE: You must tell him!

CATHY: No. No. It's my problem.

DEIDRE: Would he think it a problem?

CATHY: No. He's asked me to marry him and go to America.

DEIDRE: What did you say?

CATHY: What kind of a daft question is that? I'm already married!

DEIDRE: There's divorce.

CATHY: Now wouldn't that be grand. 'Welcome home, David. How did you enjoy prison camp? By the way do you fancy a divorce?' He's Mikey's father!

DEIDRE: Mikey can't even remember him! Stop playing the bloody martyr! Did the nuns get to you after all?

CATHY: Don't make me weaken.

DEIDRE: The war'll be over soon. Do you really want to carry on with David where you both left off?

CATHY: Do you, with Eddie?

DEIDRE: I couldn't be bringing two kids up alone. What man would want a woman with another man's child?

CATHY: Leo would. He told me so.

DEIDRE: Jesus! Then he is serious.

CATHY: If only the war had happened three years earlier, I could have met him first. We could have been happy.

DEIDRE: Don't rush, Cathy. You still have a week to think about it.

CATHY: But don't you see? Leo could be killed on his next mission. Then where would I be? He lost three of his best friends last week! No. If I put it off, I won't go ahead with it.

DEIDRE: Talk to Leo first.

CATHY: I daren't. He'd want me to have this child.

DEIDRE: All right then, but it'll cost. Twenty pounds. Because if he's caught, it's prison.

CATHY: Where the hell am I going to get money like that?

DEIDRE: We'll have a whip-round amongst the girls.

CATHY: I'll make it up to you.

MOLLY (*voice off*): Great news!

Enter MOLLY.

CATHY: And what would the great news be?

MOLLY: I've found a bloke!

DEIDRE: God alive! She's seen the light at last! And what's he like in bed?

MOLLY: Not for me! The eagle has landed. We've got Nora's bloke. He wants to meet her!

DEIDRE: Ah the poor bastard!

MOLLY: Let me read you. It's on headed notepaper.

DEIDRE: That's awful expensive stuff, that!

MOLLY: From Golders Green.

CATHY: She's dead lucky to find a Catholic there.

DEIDRE: Read it! Read it!

MOLLY: 'Dear 'Heart of Gold', I found your advertisement in the

Islington Gazette wonderfully honest and to the point....' Well done, Catherine!

DEIDRE (*crossing herself*): God forgive us for our sins!

MOLLY: 'With great economy of words, you have encapsulated...'

DEIDRE: Oh, an educated man!

MOLLY: 'Encapsulated precisely those qualities and aspirations I myself seek in a partner. I am willing to meet, should you feel so disposed...'

CATHY: Doesn't the man write well! With eloquence.

MOLLY: 'Some things, however, you ought to know about me in case they might affect your decision. I am short. Only Five foot two, and completely bald.' Behave, yourself Catherine! Listen on. 'I was born... in Germany...'

DEIDRE: A bloody Gerry! It gets worse.

MOLLY: 'But I was forced to leave, being also a Jew.'

DEIDRE: Now she'll definitely kill us!

MOLLY: 'However, I no longer attend synagogue because I have lost my faith in God... after... my whole... family....' It's so sad. All of them killed in some camp....

Silence.

CATHY: The poor man!

DEIDRE (*in despair*): And now he meets Nora!

MOLLY: 'I am, by profession, a chartered accountant...'

CATHY and DEIDRE: A Chartered accountant?!

DEIDRE: Gimme the letter! I'll marry him myself.

MOLLY: Control yourself, Deidre! Then he gives the time and place to meet – Wheelers restaurant!

DEIDRE: Wheelers! That's where the fillum stars eat.

CATHY: That lucky bitch!

DEIDRE: Wait now, he hasn't seen her yet.

CATHY: She could still have a chance. Don't they say a man should always marry someone worse lookin' than himself. Then he can't be jealous.

MOLLY: Sorry, Catherine? Your logic has me beat. So, who's going to tell Nora? It has to be soon.

DEIDRE: Well, we're a bit tied up, aren't we Cathy.

CATHY (*defensively*): I have to go to hospital. For a check up.

An uneasy silence.

MOLLY (*gives a knowing look*): I see. Then I'll do it. (*She stands.*) Here Catherine, take this. It's not much but it's a help.

CATHY looks from one to the other.

MOLLY: Hope it all goes well.

DEIDRE: I had to tell her, Cathy.

MOLLY stuffs some money into CATHY's hands, not making much of it.

Fade.

Scene Nine – A Stranger at the Threshold

CATHY is lying on the sofa, covered with a blanket. She is in some pain. She picks up a walking stick and knocks hard on the floor.

CATHY (*shouts*): Lottie! Lottie! Is that you? Can you come in, a minute!

LOTTIE: Wassup? My Gawd. You don't look well at all.

CATHY: Would you mind passing the aspirin from the table? And some water to swallow it?

LOTTIE (*does so*): How long you bin like this? You should've called me earlier.

CATHY: I'm awful sorry to trouble you.

LOTTIE: Ain't no trouble. 'Ere, get these dahn you.

CATHY (*swallows*): I've been losing blood in the night.

LOTTIE: Then you ought to git the doctor.

CATHY: No, no Lottie. No doctor. I haven't the money to pay him.

LOTTIE: Then I'll pay. It's no problem.

CATHY: Thanks Lottie, but he'd only be asking questions.

LOTTIE: Oh, I see. Like that is it? When?

CATHY: Yesterday I had it done.

LOTTIE: If he's a proper doctor, call him!

CATHY: It's more than my life's worth! He made me swear to secrecy. I don't even know his name or address.

LOTTIE: I know the type. They make a good livin' on it, too.

Leeches!

CATHY: I had to do it, Lottie.

LOTTIE: None of my business, is it? 'Ad it done meself, once. Before I was married, like. We've all bin there.

CATHY: Believe me it wasn't an easy decision.

LOTTIE: Never is, is it? Taking a life. 'Cos you never know if you're going to regret it.

CATHY: I don't want to think about it.

LOTTIE: Can I get you anyfing? Summat to eat?

CATHY: I couldn't eat a thing. Anyway, Deidre'll be back from work later. She'll do me a tin of soup.

LOTTIE: I got a drop o' brandy, if you'd like. It helps me sleep. Only, when Ern's on nights, like.

CATHY: No thanks. That stuff burns me throat.

LOTTIE: How's the boy?

CATHY: Back home next weekend, now the bombs have eased off. I'm glad he's not here to see me like this. Please God the war'll be over soon. They say it's only weeks away.

LOTTIE: It's never over till it's over.

CATHY: I've got so as I can't even imagine what it'll be like to have the men all home again.

LOTTIE: There's gonna be some changes, Kaff, you know that? Not like the last time. It's gonna be different. When we git this lot out – Mr Churchill and 'is gang.

CATHY: But he's done a fine job.

LOTTIE: In war time, yes, I grant you. But we want somethin' better. A Government that cares about us ordinary people.

CATHY: Oh politics! I'm not a one for politics.

LOTTIE: How you feelin' now?

CATHY: Better already. The aspirins are working. I think I'm over the worst.

Three loud, sharp knocks from the front door below.

LOTTIE: Who the bloody 'ell's that, this time o' mornin! Enough to waken the dead! Better go and see.

We hear LOTTIE descend quickly and return slowly up the stairs. CATHY, meanwhile, plumps up her pillow and adjusts the blanket. She picks up a novel and begins to read. The door swings open, slowly, and LOTTIE stands there, pale and trembling. In her hands she holds a letter and a telegram. CATHY closes her book and places it down. LOTTIE trudges, trance-like, to the sofa and hands CATHY the letter.

CATHY: David's handwriting. Thank God for the Red Cross! What's the other one?

LOTTIE holds out the telegram. CATHY suddenly becomes anguished.

CATHY: For me? (*She reads the address.*) Oh, it's for you, Lottie.

CATHY hands it back to LOTTIE. LOTTIE takes a step back, shakes her head and refuses to take it. Silence. CATHY glances at the telegram again.

CATHY: The War Office. Today's date. It's probably nothing at all. C'mon take it. (*Long pause.*) You're going to have to open it at some time. Go on, it'll put your mind at rest.

LOTTIE gestures for CATHY to open the telegram.

LOTTIE: Read it for me.

CATHY (*softly*): No, Lottie. I couldn't. I... it just isn't right.

LOTTIE takes the telegram and trudges away, holding it at a distance.

CATHY (*calls after LOTTIE, with concern*): Perhaps wait till Big Ern comes home?

LOTTIE exits. CATHY, troubled and thoughtful, tears open her own letter and begins to read aloud.

CATHY: 'Dear Cathy, every day that passes, I love you more and more and always will...'

CATHY breaks into silent tears. Suddenly there is an unearthly, anguished, wail from LOTTIE on the stairs outside.

LOTTIE: No. No. No. No. Noooooo! My Little Ern! Oh no!

CATHY rushes from her sofa and out to the landing.

Blackout.

Scene Ten – The Tea-Leaves Post-Mortem

CATHY is lying on the sofa with a blanket over her legs.

NEWSREADER: This is the BBC Home Service. Here is the six o'clock news for today, the twentieth of March. Allied forces in the west continue to make advances into Germany. In the east, Marshall Zhukov's forces have issued disturbing reports of mounds of bodies, numbering many thousand, in a camp in the town of Auschwitz....

Enter DEIDRE.

CATHY (*sombre*): Switch that bloody thing off. I can't bear to listen.

DEIDRE switches off wireless.

DEIDRE: How are you feeling? No more blood?

CATHY: Not since this morning.

DEIDRE: Isn't it great! We're winning in Germany!

CATHY: Nobody's winning. We're all losing. You haven't heard?

DEIDRE: Heard what?

CATHY: Little Ern. Killed in action.

DEIDRE (*holds her hand to her mouth*): Oh my God! Oh no! What desperate news! Where?

CATHY: Somewhere on the German border. Lottie got the telegram this morning. I heard this... awful scream.

DEIDRE: How is the poor woman?

CATHY: Destroyed! She's been wanderin' about like a ghost. The doctor put her on some big pills.

DEIDRE: Did you talk to her yet?

CATHY: I was here when she opened it. It was awful.

DEIDRE: She worshipped that boy.

CATHY: And I keep thinking of all the terrible things I said about him. How was I to know this would happen?

DEIDRE: There, you mustn't blame yourself. You didn't start this war.

CATHY: And Big Ern's still up in Scotland. This news'll kill him. Wait now, I'll fetch some tea.

CATHY rises. DEIDRE forces her back, gently.

CATHY: There's some still warm in the pot.

DEIDRE: Don't you dare move from that couch!

DEIDRE brings in the tea.

DEIDRE: Here y'are. This'll have you right in no time.

They sip in silence.

DEIDRE: It hasn't sunk in, yet. Poor Little Ern! Cathy, do you remember, it was before Christmas and you read the tea-leaves for me...

CATHY: Oh that. I made it all up! No tea-leaves today. I'm not in the mood.

DEIDRE: I know, but do you remember what you saw?

CATHY: No. Remind me.

DEIDRE: You saw it all.

CATHY: Nothing of the sort!

DEIDRE: You did. You saw a cradle and I asked was there a baby in it and you said you couldn't be sure, but when you looked again there was no baby.

CATHY: Did I say that?

DEIDRE: I thought it was a warning to me but...

CATHY: You're getting it all mixed up.

DEIDRE: No. Because then you said there was someone. And I remember it clearly. Someone with a name beginning with 'E', in a reclining position, as if he were asleep or something. And I thought you meant my Eddie, but...

CATHY: Oh my God. I didn't, did I?

DEIDRE: You remember now, don't you?

CATHY: I remember. Throw this tea away. I can't drink it! I swear I'll never read the tea-leaves again. I feel as if I made this all happen.

DEIDRE: Now, now. Don't be upsettin' yourself. It was all a coincidence.

CATHY: Two coincidences.

DEIDRE: But the third one – the engagement ring, the wedding. That didn't happen did it?

CATHY: No. I suppose not.

DEIDRE: There, then! Don't be getting all het up about it.

Fade.

Scene Eleven – Making up Nora

Inter-scene, we hear the news broadcast, voice over. It is evening.

NEWSREADER (*voice over*): During the night, eight hundred four-engined Lancaster bombers and four hundred American B17's of the combined RAF and US airforce carried out heavy raids on Dresden and other German cities. The governments of Peru and Chile have declared war on Germany....

Fade up.

CATHY, DEIDRE and MOLLY are busy laying out the make-up. NORA is expected.

DEIDRE: Fantastic! Gerry will be shitting his pants now the Peruvians are coming. Where is Peru, anyway?

MOLLY: South America.

CATHY: By the time they get here, they'll have missed the war altogether!

DEIDRE: Sharp lads! Now why didn't we think of that!

CATHY: Can you imagine? They'd all be riding into battle on llamas!

MOLLY: Now. Have we got everything? Deidre, did you bring the Max Factor?

DEIDRE: Max Factor, my arse! It's Woolworths. On the table. And I have some powerful, good scent. It's called 'Night in Tunisia!'

MOLLY: Let's hope Romeo has no sense of smell.

DEIDRE: Jewelry? What about the jewelry?

MOLLY: Don't worry. I bought some old sparklers of my grandmother's.

CATHY: Molly, did you happen to mention to Nora your man was a short, bald, German Jew?

MOLLY: It slipped my mind.

DEIDRE: God save us! There'll be hell to pay!

NORA approaches.

NORA (*voice off*): Anyone at home?

DEIDRE (*to audience*): And here comes the lovely Juliet herself!

NORA enters, wearing thick glasses. She glances around at each of the trio, in jerky, nervous movements. She wears a long mac down below the knees. Underneath, she should be already dressed in her Cinderella transformation gear.

251

NORA: Have you seen him? Is he nice?

CATHY: He sounds lovely.

NORA: Sounds? Sounds! What d'ye mean 'sounds'?

DEIDRE: He's a friend of Molly's, isn't that right Molly?

MOLLY: A friend of a friend.

NORA: What's his name?

MOLLY: Er, Nathan. But you can call him 'Nat'.

NORA: Is he some kind of mosquito or what? What kind of a name is 'Nat'?

CATHY: A Christian name. Well, sort of.

NORA: He's not a bloody Protestant?

CATHY (*eyes to heaven*): Oh, if only.

MOLLY: Ah no, nothing like that. In fact, if I'm not mistaken, he doesn't actually go to Church at all.

DEIDRE: Well never of a Sunday.

NORA: 'Tis all very mysterious this whole thing.

MOLLY: We've no more time to waste. It's six thirty and you've to meet at the restaurant at eight.

NORA: Eight! What kind of a lunatic eats at eight o'clock in the middle of the night! I'm starvin'! Cathy, do you have a crust of bread in the house?

DEIDRE (*pushing her towards the sofa*): No time for that! Lie back on the sofa!

NORA: What for?

NORA is forced back on the couch, whilst MOLLY pretends to be pulling on a surgeon's rubber gloves. She holds up her arms, ready for 'surgery'.

CATHY: It'll be good practice for you!

NORA: Mind me glasses! I'm blind without them.

DEIDRE: Tis just as well, Nora!

The trio all huddle around with MOLLY administering, CATHY and DEIDRE handing the implements to her from the table, like surgeon's assistants. They form a wall around NORA so the audience cannot see the quick change. (In fact, they are removing NORA's mac, mask and glasses.)

CATHY: Here, slip this dress on you. And these!

MOLLY: Right, and now... foundation cream. Powder. Rouge! (*Each is passed down the line.*)

DEIDRE: Is it working?

MOLLY: Surprisingly well. Hold still Nora! Lipstick! Pout your lips, woman!

NORA: I am pouting them.

MOLLY: Well, where are they then? I can't see them.

DEIDRE: There! It's that razor slash underneath the nose.

MOLLY: Ah, I see them now! Now for the eyes. Don't you know the eyes are the windows of the soul? Pass the eye shadow!

CATHY: Easy on the eye shadow! The eyes way back in her head.

NORA: Ow!

MOLLY: We need a longer eye pencil. This one can't reach!

DEIDRE: Let me have a go. Close your eyes! Nora! Close them!

NORA: They are closed!

DEIDRE: So they are. Keep them closed. Good. Good. There now. How's that?

NORA: I can't see a bloody thing!

MOLLY (*calmly, taking over again*): Open them. There. Right, up you get!

NORA rises from the couch, beautifully dressed and bejewelled. She is, of course, a perfectly good looking actress, but to the audience it will seem a transformation. She stretches out her arms and twirls around.

NORA: How do I look?

DEIDRE: You'll do! You're not a bad looking girl at all!

CATHY (*emotional*): Oh Nora. You look beautiful!

NORA: Do you mean that?

MOLLY: 'We have done God's work here this night!'

CATHY: Oh! Look at the time. Cinderella, you'll be late for the ball!

NORA: Why don't you all come with me, till I clap eyes on him?

MOLLY: I think not, Nora.

DEIDRE: Oh, to hell with it! Let's get her a taxi!

NORA: A taxi? A real taxi all to myself?

CATHY: Why not! She's worth it, isn't she girls?

ALL: Yes. Good Luck!

NORA: Oh, Oh I'm going to cry!

DEIDRE: Don't you dare! There's a year's supply of make-up gone into this operation.

MOLLY: Come on. We'll see you to the taxi rank.

The happy party departs.

Fade.

Scene Twelve – And a Nightingale Sang in Berkeley Square

Front of stage left, a table for two, with white tablecloth, two wine glasses and ice bucket. NATHAN, in lounge suit, collar and tie, sits reading a book. He wears glasses. He checks his watch. A WAITRESS in uniform approaches from wings right, with order book. NATHAN shrugs again and checks his watch. The WAITRESS turns and walks back, slowly. It is important both NORA and NATHAN are wearing thick, horn-rimmed spectacles. Enter NORA, right, in full regalia, like a short-sighted heron approaching a trout farm. She peers over the WAITRESS's shoulder, sees NATHAN, who has risen to greet her. NORA, losing her nerve, turns hurriedly on her heels. The WAITRESS, smiling, takes NORA's arm, gently, and guides her towards NATHAN. The WAITRESS slips the overcoat from NORA's shoulders, before departing with it.

NORA (*over her shoulder*): Keep an eye on that coat! I wouldn't want it be stolen or anythin'. It's not mine!

NATHAN smiles, gives a short, dignified bow of the head and offers his hand. He has a slight German accent, with overtones of American and cultivated.

NATHAN: Nathan Blumberg! Miss O'Rourke, I presume?

NORA (*shakes*): Ye Wha? Oh! (*Smiles.*) The name's Nora.

NATHAN *slides her chair out for her, gentlemanly. NORA is flustered at such attention, gawps and, finally, sits. NATHAN slides her chair in.*

NATHAN (*pouring, casually, from the napkinned bottle*): Some champagne?

NORA: Champagne? Jesus!

NATHAN: You do drink wine?

NORA: I'll give it a go! (*She knocks back a whole glass and splutters.*)

NATHAN (*amused*): But slowly, huh! It's a good year. (*Checking the bottle.*)

NORA: Not bad for April. Apart from the rain. D'ye mind if I smoke? I'm gaspin'!

NATHAN *calmly offers one from his cigarette case. They both light up.*

NORA (*checking the brand*): Never tried these fellahs before. Are they foreign?

NATHAN: American.

NORA: Ah, I thought I detected a bit of an accent there. I'm very sharp on the accents.

NATHAN: So. We're both foreigners. You are an Irish lady?

NORA: Ireland, yes. Kilkenny.

NATHAN: Irish women are noted for their fine complexions. It's true, I see.

NORA (*warming*): Ah, come on now, will ye. I know I'm no Venus.

NATHAN: So, I'm no Adonis! My brother had the looks. I got the brains.

NORA: Well I'm not short in that department, meself.

NATHAN: And what about your Irish writers, huh? James Joyce. 'Ulysses'. Such a book!

NORA: God, I wouldn't be readin' stuff like that. It's a dirty book.

NATHAN: Who says so?

NORA: The Holy Father. And he ought to know.

NATHAN: Why? Has he read it?

NORA: You know that's a very good question. I suppose he must have.

NATHAN: If it's good enough for the Pope, it's good enough for you. Read! Enjoy!

NORA: Right enough. By the way, what happened to the hair?

NATHAN (*momentarily defensive, then he laughs*): My hair? Oh. It just... fell out. I didn't ask it why. Is it a problem?

NORA: Not at all. It's very... manly. I see you have the thick specs like meself. Can I try them on? Here you try mine! We'll see who has the worst eyesight.

They exchange spectacles, playfully.

NATHAN: You know, it's very strange. I can see you more clearly with your glasses.

NORA: And me with yours! You're a good lookin' fellah! (*They return the spectacles.*) So, Nathan, where are you from?

NATHAN: For five years I lived in New York. Originally, from

Austria. Vienna.

NORA: Oh, so you speak Austrian, then?

NATHAN: German. Austrians are German.

NORA: German! God save us! I think I need another drink. (*She helps herself.*)

NATHAN: Relax. Don't worry. These days I never speak German. It's a point of principle.

NORA (*gulping down the champagne*): Thank God for that. Everybody'd be gawpin' at us.

NATHAN: I thought I'd explained all this in the letter.

NORA: Letter? What letter?

NATHAN: My reply to your advertisement. If you did not receive it, how did you know to meet me here?

NORA: Those divils! So, you're not a friend of Molly's?

NATHAN (*a good-natured shrug*): 'Molly'? This person I don't know. Who's Molly?

NORA: An old school friend. Just wait till I see her next! I'm not in the habit of advertisin' meself, like an oul' gas cooker or somethin'! The cheek!

NATHAN (*laughs*): So! This 'Molly' arranged our meeting without telling you, already?

NORA: It must be her idea of a joke.

NATHAN: A 'joke'?

NORA: Oh please. Don't be offended, Nathan. I mean, here we both are, in a lovely restaurant. The laugh's on them. Can we eat? I'm starved.

NATHAN: The fish is very good here.

NORA: Ah, no. Not fish. The convent put me off fish for life. Every Friday – boiled fish, poached fish, fish-cakes! Do they do boiled bacon, at all?

NATHAN signals to the WAITRESS.

NATHAN (*to WAITRESS*): We'll have the soup to start, please. I'll have the plaice and the lady... (*he whispers in the WAITRESS's ear*) and another bottle of the same!

WAITRESS departs.

NORA: Posh place, eh? (*Whispers.*) I've never been waited on before.

NATHAN: So this is your first time?

NORA: First time in a restaurant!

NATHAN: What kind of man, who doesn't take you out?

NORA: No kind of man.

NATHAN: You mean I am your first date?

NORA (*backtracking*): Oh I've been asked, hundreds of times, you know, but I'm... very choosy.

NATHAN: Choosy is a good way to be.

NORA: You're right. But it's... very lonely.

NATHAN: Tell me about 'lonely'. Have you no family?

NORA: Not a soul. I was an orphan child. Brought up in an institution till I was eighteen. My father was killed in the troubles and my mother... died of TB. I could only have been about six, I think. I can barely remember.

NATHAN: Then Nora, we have much in common.

NORA: No family?

NATHAN: Oh, I had a family. A huge family in Vienna. My parents, a brother, three sisters, uncles and aunts I couldn't count. I even had a great grandmother.

NORA: So where are they all?

NATHAN (*visibly upset*): After the Anschluss, I... am the only one to survive.

A long pause.

NORA: God almighty! How awful!

NATHAN (*nods*): I was eighteen at the time. My father had sent me and my brother to Switzerland. He knew what was coming. From there – America.

NORA: So what happened to your brother?

NATHAN: He joined the American air force. They wouldn't take me. Poor eyesight. He was killed in action. In Norfolk. I came back here for the funeral. I stayed. To be near him, I suppose.

NORA (*she reaches across the table*): You poor man.

NATHAN: For a while, I sank myself in work. But a man cannot just live for his work. It's not enough.

NORA: Nathan, are you religious at all?

NATHAN: Your friends obviously didn't tell you.

NORA: That you're Jewish? You'd have to be after what you've just told me.

NATHAN: I don't go to synagogue. Not any more. It's hard to believe in anything in such times we live in.

NORA: Do you mind if I ask you something?

NATHAN: Ask!

NORA: What did the girls say about me in the advertisement?

NATHAN: Nice things. Good things. That you have lovely skin.

NORA: What else?

NATHAN: That you have a 'heart of gold'.

NORA (*wipes away a tear*): Really? Did they say that?

NATHAN: You have very perceptive friends. You can tell much about a person who has such friends.

NORA: Anything else?

NATHAN: It doesn't matter. A small thing! I don't want that I should embarrass you.

NORA: Tell me, please. I want to know.

NATHAN: They said you wanted... marriage. And a family.

NORA (*warmly*): I have no secrets at all, then! Terrible girls!

NATHAN: No, clever girls! Wise girls! Let's drink to them.

NORA: To Molly, Deidre and Cathy!

NATHAN: Molly, Deidre and Cathy!

Fade.

Scene Thirteen – Love Conquers All

CATHY, DEIDRE and MOLLY scramble through the door of Cathy's flat and rush to the wireless.

DEIDRE: It can't be true!

MOLLY: It's just a rumour!

CATHY: It is true. A whole bus queue can't be wrong!

DEIDRE: Quick then and switch it on.

MOLLY: Hurry Catherine! We'll miss it!

CATHY: Shush now! Don't rush me!

CATHY switches on wireless.

NEWSREADER: It has just been announced from Downing Street, that Hitler is dead...

CATHY: There! Didn't I tell you!

DEIDRE: The old bastard! Dead!

MOLLY: Shush! Quiet!

NEWSREADER: At eleven o'clock this morning, Greenwich Mean Time, the Prime Minister, Mr Winston Churchill, broke to the world the news of the death of the German Führer....

The three women embrace and whoop excitedly.

MOLLY: It's over!

DEIDRE: Peace at last!

CATHY: Wait! Be quiet, will you?

NEWSREADER: More prison camps have been released by advancing allied forces...

DEIDRE: I'd better go home and tidy up!

CATHY: Shut up!

NEWSREADER: They are Stalag Luft Four and Six. Stalag Eleven, A and B...

CATHY (*stunned, holding hands to forehead*): I think they said Stalag Eleven B had been released.

CATHY (*excited*): That's David's camp. David's camp has been released!

She claps her hand to her mouth in disbelief. MOLLY and DEIDRE embrace CATHY. They all kiss each other, whooping and shouting. CATHY switches off the wireless. All three flop into sofa or chairs, apart from each other. After the initial excitement, a strange silence sets in.

CATHY: David – coming home!

DEIDRE: And my Eddie – coming home!

MOLLY (*slightly subdued*): Well now, isn't this something to celebrate!

CATHY and DEIDRE look at each other. Their expressions change.

DEIDRE: But what'll I tell Joe?

CATHY: And what'll I say to Leo?

MOLLY: 'Good-bye!' is what you'll say to the pair of them.

DEIDRE (*sadly*): I'll have to give up the job!

CATHY: Me too! No more American Legion!

MOLLY: Of course! You've husbands and children to look after now. Isn't that what you've always wanted?

DEIDRE: I'll miss it though. I'll really miss it!

CATHY: Me too! It was great fun while it lasted.

MOLLY: It wasn't fun for David and Eddie.

CATHY: Well I know that, Molly, for God's sake! But still...

MOLLY: But still what?

DEIDRE: What she means is, well, four years is a long time. They could be different people!

CATHY: Or the same people.

MOLLY: Which is it you fear most, that they're the same or different?

CATHY: I know what Deidre means!

DEIDRE: Yes, don't be asking stupid questions Molly. God, you put a damper on everything!

MOLLY: You should be happy, the pair of you!

CATHY (*starts to cry*): I am happy! (*Embraces DEIDRE.*)

DEIDRE (*also tearful*): I'm happy too. See. Now you've the pair of us in tears.

CATHY: You don't understand.

DEIDRE: You've never been married.

MOLLY: So, here we go. My fault now, is it, that you've two fine men to be welcoming home? Think of Lottie – no homecomings for her!

CATHY (*smartening up*): She's right Deidre. We've got to stop this. We're being silly.

MOLLY: If anyone's anything to be sad about, it's me.

CATHY: What do you mean by that?

MOLLY: You'll hardly want an oul' spinster hanging about the place when your men get back, now will you?

CATHY: Molly, you'll always be welcome.

DEIDRE: Yes. You can still come round – like old times.

CATHY: Mikey adores you.

MOLLY: He's just a kid! The sad thing is... no, I mustn't say it! (*She becomes pensive as they brighten up.*)

CATHY: What is it Molly? You can tell us.

MOLLY: Not this. No. I can't.

DEIDRE: We're your friends. You can tell us anything.

There is a pause as MOLLY decides.

MOLLY: This last few weeks... have been the happiest in my whole life.

CATHY: Go on.

MOLLY: I've been... seeing somebody.

DEIDRE: Do we know this... person?

MOLLY: No. A captain in the American army.

DEIDRE: So far, so good.

MOLLY: The women's army.

DEIDRE: Uh-oh!

CATHY: Is she nice?

MOLLY: Well, you know, a bit... military. But underneath she's a real sweetie!

DEIDRE: Underneath what, for God's sake?

CATHY: Shut up, Deidre! Go on tell us. What's her name?

MOLLY: Vivienne. Isn't it awful. I haven't been able to tell anybody. I'm not even sure I should be telling you.

DEIDRE: I've known for years. Well, not about her!

MOLLY: But that's it, don't you see! I can't hide it any more.

CATHY: Well, you're going to have to hide it, love. That kind of thing doesn't go down too well.

DEIDRE: Unless you're in the theatre or something. They're all a bit queer in that profession.

MOLLY: Thanks Deidre. You're a straight talker, if nothin' else.

DEIDRE: If it's making you unhappy, perhaps you ought to think again.

MOLLY: God woman, have you never been in love!

DEIDRE: Talk sense, woman! You can't actually love her like I love Eddie or Cathy loves David?

MOLLY: Oh much more than that! I couldn't even look at another woman.

DEIDRE: Point taken!

CATHY: Touché! I hope it all works out for you.

DEIDRE: Yes things'll all change for the better now the war's over.

CATHY: There'll be no going back to the old days. We'll all be together again. There'll be food on the table.

DEIDRE: Coal on the fire and street lights...

CATHY: Houses for us to live in – new ones!

DEIDRE: And jobs for us all and holidays at the seaside! Think of it!

CATHY: And bananas and oranges...

DEIDRE: And chocolate. Don't forget the chocolate. God what I wouldn't do for a whole bar of it – the silver paper and those lovely wrappers...

CATHY: Steak, Deidre, do you remember steak?

DEIDRE: We'll all be eating like Americans!

CATHY: And fashions. We can all dress like women again, not those awful bloody slacks and jackets with shoulders like a prizefighter!

MOLLY: But I like dressing this way!

DEIDRE: So you do! No offence Molly!

CATHY: There'll be sugar and real butter again and milk and honey. It'll be like the promised land!

MOLLY: But no Vivienne!

DEIDRE: She'll get leave! You can see her on leave!

NORA *approaches on the stairs.*

NORA (*voice off*): Girls! Girls! I want a word with you? You devils, you!

DEIDRE: Bloody hell! It's Nora. Lock the door, quick. Pretend we're not here!

MOLLY: No. We have to face her! I'll take the blame. It was my idea.

CATHY: Are you mad? She'll murder us all! (*She rushes to lock the door.*)

NORA strides in before it can be locked. She is playing a game with them, feigning seriousness.

NORA: So, here you all are, the witches' coven!

CATHY: Nora, we're awful sorry.

DEIDRE: 'Twas just a bit of a laugh, that's all!

NORA advances on MOLLY.

NORA: So, 'a friend of a friend' was he?

MOLLY: He sounded like a nice fellah, by all accounts.

NORA: Well I hope you're all feeling proud of yourselves. Haven't you heard the great news?

CATHY: You mean, Hitler's dead?

DEIDRE: Yes, it was just on the wireless.

NORA: No, not that. This!

NORA thrusts out her hand with an engagement ring on her finger.

MOLLY: God alive! An engagement ring!

CATHY: Jesus! It's a miracle. It's gorgeous!

DEIDRE: Just like you saw in the tea-leaves, Cathy! Will you get a load of that!

MOLLY: Congratulations Nora O'Rourke. So you hit it off with him. I thought you would.

NORA: He's the kindest, sweetest, loveliest man in the whole world, so he is.

DEIDRE: But surely you can't marry a Jew. What would Sister Murphy say?

NORA: Sister Murphy can go screw herself!

CATHY: Come on. Let's see that ring again.

NORA displays the ring.

CATHY: I have... always... wanted... a ring... like that!

Playfully, CATHY lunges at the ring and horseplay ensues.

CATHY: Gimme that ring! Come on girls let's have the ring off her! We worked hard for that!

They all join the tussle.

NORA: Stoppit. No. It's mine. You're not getting it.

They retreat backstage in a rolling maul, as the NARRATOR/ MICKEY steps forward. They make silent conversation backstage, over what follows.

NARRATOR/MIKEY: And that was how my mother and Deidre and Molly and Nora defeated Hitler's plans for a master-race of supermen. She used to tell me it was when Hitler got the message of Nora's engagement to Nathan Blumberg that he knew the game was up and blew out his excuse for a brain. I have never seen any reason to doubt that. And poor Lottie! She made the ultimate sacrifice of her only son, that we might live. I kissed goodbye to the stuffed owl, my grandmother's wart and the parsley soup with bones. The father I didn't know returned, and I went to see the King and Queen at the Victory celebrations. And what of Nora and Nathan? Why, they lived... happily ever after.

NATHAN enters and joins NORA arm in arm. THE GIRLS press forward, throwing confetti. LOTTIE watches, sadly.

The End.

MARK JENKINS

In Conversation With

HAZEL WALFORD DAVIES

Hazel Walford Davies: Apart from *Playing Burton*, the plays published here find their book form for the first time. It is an occasion for congratulations in which all interested in theatre in Wales and beyond will want to join.

Mark Jenkins: Thank you! I would certainly like to think of this volume of plays as a form of recognition by my peers, people 'in the business' of drama here in Wales. It is gratifying, but in an entirely different way to hearing an audience break into applause after a performance. I have worked to make a sustained contribution to theatre over a period of twenty years. For many years, I had to rely on London productions to get my work professionally performed. I'm glad that that dependence is now slowly beginning to change.

HWD: Your emphasis on a point of gravity here in Wales is interesting. Could you expand on that?

MJ: You don't have to look far to see the reasons for my late arrival at the Welsh dramatists' ball. For a start, I am a born-and-bred Londoner. I'm also half-Irish, and my Welsh 'half' has a fair mix of Scots in it. On the other hand, my father's first language was Welsh and he had six brothers and sisters, most of whom had to move to London to find work. So Christmases in London were bilingual festivals: the aunts and uncles conversing in Welsh at one end of the room and their non-Welsh spouses and all us kids speaking English at the other end. My Irish mother was an orphan, so we had no Irish relatives at all. I also went to school in Wales for a couple of years, but since most of the school kids were English evacuees, the teaching was in English. Now that I've lived in Cardiff for almost twenty-five years, I'm as Welsh (whatever that means) as I've ever been. I spend a good deal of time in Pembrokeshire, especially at St David's, but Pembrokeshire, too, as you know, is a county with a split personality.

HWD: 'As Welsh as I've ever been' – how would you say the Welsh connection has impacted on your work?

MJ: Only two of my plays are truly Welsh – *Playing Burton* and *Mr Owen's Millennium*. But, again, both Richard Burton and Robert Owen were globe-trotting internationalists, who made their homes and careers abroad. Only recently has it occurred to me that most of my work tends to be about people living away from where they 'belong'. *Birthmarks* is about Germans exiled in Soho; *Downtown Paradise* is the story of a Jewess and a black-American in San Francisco; and *Nora's Bloke* is about Irishwomen in north London. Not included in this present volume are two other published plays *Strindberg Knew My Father* (Swedish people exiled in Denmark) and *Rosebud* (American Orson Welles exiled from Hollywood). Likewise my first feature film, *The Scarlet Tunic*, was a love story about a German soldier and an English woman, set in the West country. A little surprisingly, such subject matter didn't sit well with the 'new Wales' theatrical agenda that was emerging in the 1980s and 1990s.

HWD: Certainly surprising, as you say. Can I ask if the surely international relevance, currency and resonance of the theme – that of 'people living away from where they "belong"' – has engaged a little more with tastes abroad? If so, to what extent and to what effect?

MJ: Undoubtedly it has been the international success of *Playing Burton* that has won me recognition. This is its second Welsh publication by Parthian Books. And now the play is part of the inaugural season of the new Wales Millennium Centre in the Bay. It will run for twenty-one performances, opening in December 2004, and is currently being translated into Swedish, Norwegian, Danish and Icelandic for a three-year Scandinavian performance contract. Prior to this it will have had three Edinburgh fringe seasons and two extensive runs in London as well as tours of England and Scotland and outings in Wales. It has played at the Israeli festival in Jerusalem and the Budapest festival. It toured New Zealand in 2002, winning, I'm glad to say, for the Welsh New Zealander actor Ray Henwood the prestigious Chapman-Tripp Award. It toured Australia in 2003, most notably for two weeks at the Sydney Opera House. In New York in the autumn of 2003, it was pleasing that the six-week off-Broadway run had to be extended to ten weeks to meet demand.

HWD: This widespread simultaneous exposure of a contemporary Welsh play is certainly remarkable. As far as I can see, at one point in 2003 three different actors were playing the role simultaneously on three continents, whilst a fourth was performing it in front of Anthony Sher and the assembled Royal Shakespeare Company at the Swan Theatre in Stratford-upon-Avon.

MJ: Performances number an estimated eight hundred over twelve years; an average of sixty a year, with 150 in 2003. I naturally find it odd that during that time *Playing Burton* never had more than about three one-night stands in Cardiff, the city where I live and work, and was not long ago turned down for a season at the Sherman Theatre. The international acclaim pleases me because it is for a Welsh play about one of the greatest Welshmen of modern times; by a Welshman-in-residence; acted mostly by a Welshman, Josh Richards; directed and often produced by a Welshman, Guy Masterson, Burton's great nephew, after all. Hardly a gamble, I would have thought.

HWD: And yet it has taken the arrival in Cardiff of an Australian, Judith Isherwood, as Chief Executive of the WMC, finally to secure recognition of the play in the Welsh capital. What, in short, are your feelings about that?

MJ: 'Thank God for Australians'? Surely there is some kind of lesson here for those of us concerned with theatre in Wales. One lesson is this – the small unassuming door, the one closest to the writer, is the hardest one to enter, whereas on the other side of the planet the imposing portals of the Sydney Opera House are open. It's an irony, and I believe I know why. Theatrical gatekeepers in this neck of the woods have been laying down 'agendas' for Welsh writers and have been busy outlining 'collective' visions for Welsh theatre. All this, instead of listening or reading. Why not read the scripts our younger writers come up with, instead of harnessing them to target dwindling minority audiences. Theatre is already under the choking market pressure of television and film; the last thing it needs is to be ghetto-ised. Why, then, the massive cultural bias amongst the gatekeepers against mainstream theatre? Positive discrimination rightly promotes 'women's' theatre', 'gay theatre', 'physical theatre', 'experimental theatre', 'ethnic minority theatre' and 'theatre for the disabled'. Why is it not right also to promote 'theatre-for–all'?

HWD: You touch there not only on what is a funding-led, treasury-led situation, but a 'thematically-led' regime as well . . .

MJ: I'm in favour of all sectors having free access to make their contribution to theatre at large. That's the point. I would like to think that I do practise what I preach. *Downtown Paradise* is an example. It's set in San Francisco, anything but on my own doorstep. The protagonist is a woman, like my mother, my sister, and my partner (the two sexes have a long history of mutual interaction). Rachel is a Jewish lawyer who takes on a black client, James, a prison convict, charged with the murder of a prison guard. She falls in love with him. Both of them have human failings, which are tested to destruction in the course of the drama. Rachel idealises her black lover. She believes him to be innocent, though she knows he is no saint. Half way through the play, there is an assassination attempt on Rachel and she is left in a wheelchair for the rest of her life. Disillusioned with men in general, she becomes a feminist. She also takes a woman lover in an attempt to find happiness and love. But the mistakes of her past return to haunt her.

HWD: It's a play with the power to shock and move audiences, and I can see that it makes no concessions to prejudice of any kind. Indeed, I can't think of a minority audience that would find it anything but inclusive.

MJ: But I didn't consciously set out to 'include' them. It's about life, it's about people, not 'categories' or 'minorities'. I was at pains to do something without special pleading. When we were casting the James Wilson role in London, one of the black actors, auditioning for the role, asked if he could be introduced to the writer. The director pointed roughly in my direction and the guy walked right past me and vigorously shook hands with another auditioning black actor. It was the finest possible compliment because a white man should be capable of writing a convincing black role. Likewise, if a man can't write a woman's role, he should give up writing and take up bodybuilding. If a straight man can only devise comic caricatures for gay or lesbian roles, he should widen his circle of friends.

HWD: Much of what you have said is relevant to what you see as your achievement so far and your thoughts into the future. Remind us of where it all started.

MJ: My very first publication was an academic volume on Aneurin Bevan and the Bevanites, of interest today only to scholars of British post-war politics, but still in print and often quoted in other works. I have travelled a long way in terms of subject matter since I first became a playwright in the early 1980s. The play *Birthmarks* is from the same early 'political period', when I was just setting out in drama. All the same, it made its mark, winning first prize in the Drama Association of Wales national competition in 1986. But even so I had to take it to London for its first production. The second production was here in Wales and it subsequently toured to Stuttgart.

HWD: Remind us of its setting and concerns.

MJ: The initial subject matter of *Birthmarks* was the hundred-year conspiracy to conceal the identity of Karl Marx's illegitimate son. A good deal of research and a good part of my adult life up to then were a preparation for it, in terms of reading and knowledge of the subject. The piece takes place during three years in mid-nineteenth century London, and all the action occurs in the Marx family's dingy flat in a Soho that was rife at that time with typhoid. It is certainly not a 'political polemic'. It is about personal relations within the Marx circle and examines the way these German émigrés treated each other, their wives, their lovers, their 'comrades'. The backdrop is that of extreme, if self-imposed, poverty and utter dedication to the 'cause' which, at that time, was still notionally spotless and admirable.

HWD: A play, then, to quote Philip Larkin's words in another context, about 'aims long fallen wide'

MJ: Exactly, as long as we remember that these were not self-seeking hedonists but people at one stage with the purest motives. And yet, Marx gets his German house-help, Helen Demuth, pregnant. She and Engels conspire to conceal the truth from Marx's wife Jenny and from the whole world, so that the 'cause' should not be tarnished. The movement splits into vicious duelling, fist-fighting factions, children dying from deprivation and with lying and character assassination a way of life. There, in that Soho flat, only months after its founding, the DNA, as it were, of a movement that would take the world by storm (and create storms) is already in place as Marx, tormented by carbuncles and crippling headaches, begins his abstract blueprint for a happier world. The humour in the play (yes, there's plenty of that, too) arises from the vanity of men who believe themselves to be gods, and who regard life as a rehearsal for some ideal retreating future.

HWD: I'm very much taken by what you there tellingly term the 'DNA of a movement'. I've often been puzzled by the fact that the main movements of world history have had relatively ordinary, even banal, beginnings, given the individuals who impelled, propelled and compelled them. My wonder leads to the question as to why a contemporary dramatist writing in Wales in the twentieth and twenty-first centuries should still see in, say, 1917 Europe some DNA that makes for drama.

MJ: You're right. Why did I write it? By the 1980s I was convinced that the communism of my youth wasn't a viable system. I predicted its collapse in the dedication of my book on the Bevanites. By then, I had met former inmates of the gulags, whom I had the honour to help get released through Amnesty International – people such as Victor Fainberg, Anatoly Scharansky, Leonid Plyusch, Vladimir Borisov and Vladimir Bukovsky. The 'impossibility' of communism was always in the air, but I was convinced that, if it was fatally flawed now, it had probably been so from its very conception. Hence, *Birthmarks*. We don't know much about the mysterious process by which a writer chooses his subject matter. When you're engrossed in writing a play, it is the last question, certainly not the first, on your mind. Playwriting is a kind of obsessive-compulsive disorder. In my earlier dramatic writing, I was always trying just to make sense of felt experiences that I, and my generation, had lived through. For most of us, that was the era of socialist commitment. Socialism in all its various forms was the preoccupation, the guiding passion, the vision of an entire epoch. It displaced religion and became a secular substitute for it.

HWD: Then of course, in 1989, all that finally changed when the Berlin Wall came down. As it happens, the wall came dows two months after the Stuttgart production of *Birthmarks*! I risk foisting that coincidence because in 1989 I aborted a lecturing visit to the universities of Bucharest and Timisoara in Romania because my luggage was mysteriously 'lost' before take-off by Taarom Airways at Heathrow. A week later Ceausescu fell! (I hope the exclamation mark comes stinging across.) It certainly brings things home to you. But then, post-1989, social-democratic parties began to accommodate a new, sometimes a *re*newed, belief in private enterprise in all sorts of unlikely parts of the world.

MJ: I was never a mourner at the grave of abstract socialism in the first place. I do, however, mourn the passing of those tangible 'Old Labour' communities that contributed so much to working class life, morality and culture. One of my pet hates is having to listen to old, unrepentant communists justifying past steadfastness 'in the cause' with a moral certitude they would not, quite rightly, countenance lending to former Nazis. The one regime was clearly as bad as the other. The only, and unavailing, shade of difference is that we western communists were for so long apologists for an inhuman system under which only other people had to live, suffer and die.

HWD: To bring things home in another, warmer sense, remembering the Newtown, Montgomeryshire connection, let me mention the name Robert Owen.

MJ: For this relief, much thanks. Robert Owen stands in sharp contrast to the dark, brooding, quarrelsome Karl Marx. My play *Mr Owen's Millennium* is a celebration of a really wonderful human being, one who still hasn't received the recognition he deserves for his courage, vision and humanity. Owen adored children and they, him. He had a large family of his own but he cared every bit as much about the children of his factory labourers. He abolished child labour in his factories and paid for children to go to school, where music, dance and art featured prominently in the curriculum. He was a life-affirming character, exuding an optimism that was not traduced or betrayed by what were his quite revolutionary views and social innovations. Always at the centre of his vision was the welfare of working people and their families. I wrote the play because I felt Owen had acquired a totally unjustified reputation as a 'dreamer'. He had his dreams of course, but he was already an extremely practical man, generous with his time and with the great wealth he had accumulated from his decided success in the world of business. He was prepared to put his money at the service of social reform, factory reform, universal education, town planning and the abolition of child labour.

HWD: And as the subject of drama?

MJ: The term moral charisma comes to mind – along with the possibilities for interaction which that always suggests. The love Owen bestowed on others was returned to him. He was revered by his followers and his workforce. When he was a very old man, people would reach out of the crowd to touch his clothing. A child once asked 'Is this Jesus, mother?' Indeed, I would welcome the chance to adapt the Owen story as a musical, with a large cast of children for ensemble songs and dances. The story lends itself to that kind of treatment. Owen is a man all children should get to know about in schools. There aren't too many such genuinely benevolent characters in history books. And let us never forget that in Newtown he came from a relatively poor family, yet became one of the richest men in the world, only to spend his entire fortune on the welfare of others.

HWD: And to bring things even closer home, there's *Nora's Bloke*.

MJ: Yes, after the Cardiff production, the play immediately secured a second. It opens in New York City at the Blue Heron Arts Centre, off Park Avenue, in August 2004. In *Nora's Bloke*, the heroine, Cathy James, is very closely based on my own mother and her circle of Irish friends. I have dedicated this volume to my mother's memory for a number of reasons. She was a deeply spiritual person, with her feet planted firmly on the ground. I would describe her as a true pagan. Her upbringing in a Catholic orphanage left no mark on her at all, save for the love of literature and music, which she acquired there. When I was about fifteen, she fed me play scripts by Bernard Shaw, Sean O'Casey and Synge and books by Liam O'Flaherty, Flann O'Brien and James Joyce. She said I needed to prepare myself because 'You're going to be a playwright!' And even when I became an academic, writing articles on politics, she did not despair. Only as she approached her final two years of life did I suddenly feel the compulsion to write drama, and then three plays came pouring out – *Birthmarks*, *Playing Burton* and *Mr Owen's Millennium* were all completed, though not performed, before she died.

HWD: That must have been gratifying both ways, and a further tribute in the play must be its female orientation.

MJ: Yes, in *Nora's Bloke*, Cathy is an amateur clairvoyant. She reads the fortunes of her friends in the tea-leaves at the bottom of their cups. She makes three unlikely predictions and they are all fulfilled by the end of the play, but in ways that surprise her and everybody else. It's a true story. When you have a mother like Cath, you don't have to invent anything; you're always struggling to keep up with her. The stage is dominated by women – six of them. All the men are away at war and it is women who rule the 'home' front. They survive intensive rocket raids on London and struggle to come to terms with the consequences of an approaching peace.

HWD: Is that in the sense that peace, like war, sometimes breaks out?

MJ: Yes, because peace threatens the independence they have established. Humour is their independent weapon against adversity, even though it dances cheek-to-cheek with sudden, violent death. Cathy has one big decision to make when the war ends. Predictably, she chooses the option which best serves those she loves the most, and not the one her heart may have desired. In the dedication to this volume, I have given Cath back her maiden surname, because it is one I share with her. She wanted me never to forget that I am hers. As if I could!

June, 2004

REVIEW EXCERPTS

Playing Burton

'One of the most successful – possibly the most successful – Welsh plays of modern times... a remarkable monologue that has toured the world more or less constantly in the past decade.'

David Adams, Western Mail, 5 December 2003

'A haunting, indeed mesmerising one-man show, written with obvious depth of understanding... deliriously literate... an unforgettable distillation of the essence of Burton's uniqueness... Josh Richards gives a shattering portrayal!'

Jack Tinker, Daily Mail, 12 August 1994

'An exceptionally powerful and darkly haunting slice of theatre... highly lyrical and beautifully literate... faultless, riveting, brilliantly charismatic and peerlessly acted by Josh Richards.'

Dan Rider, The Scotsman, 16 August 1997

'Virtuoso writing, lyrical and rich... I had to keep reminding myself that this (Brian Mallon) was not actually Richard Burton in front of me.'

Norman Mailer, Provincetown, Cape Cod, USA, August 2002

Birthmarks

'Birthmarks succeeds brilliantly... memorable, sophisticated, intelligent... yet addressed in a fresh, colloquial manner and spiced with sexual innuendo. Performances in this award-winning play were uniformly excellent!'

Nicole Sochor, Western Mail, 26 April 1989

'Superb! A treat to watch! The best play I have seen this year.'

Mike Buckingham, South Wales Argus, 26 April 1989

Downtown Paradise

'In Mark Jenkins, Wales has a writer who has rejected the tendency to navel gaze and has taken on issues for a wider audience. See this play!'

Matt Jones, South Wales Echo, 11 May 1996

'A measured and provoking drama, confident in its craftsmanship. There are moments when the insanity of human barbarism glides darkly into view... a powerhouse of emotions.'

Kate Stratton, London Evening Standard, 19 April 1996

'Mark Jenkins takes us on a dangerous racial and sexual journey with an astute sense of time and place... Richard C Sharp gives a magnificent performance as the civil rights activist who becomes emotionally involved with his white lawyer....'

Baz Bamigboye, Daily Mail, 19 April 1996

Mr Owen's Millennium

'Robert Owen, the Newtown-born philanthropist... and grand visionary was brought to pulsing life... in this gifted outpouring... full marks to the playwright... England may have its Trevor Griffiths. We have our Mark Jenkins. 'Tis enough!'

Jon Gower, BBC Wales Arts Correspondent
New Welsh Review, #36, 1996

Nora's Bloke

'It's good to have such a great storyteller as Mark Jenkins to highlight the experiences that many of us went through... it's a good, old-fashioned, gripping... and amusing story, highlighting the bewilderment and uncertainties of wartime.'

Mike Kelligan, Theatre Wales website, 11 December 2003